IT HELPS TO BE CRAZY!

IT HELPS TO BE CRAZY!

*Anecdotes and insights from
an unlikely missionary.*

Tom Jopling

IT HELPS TO BE CRAZY!
Anecdotes and insights from an unlikely missionary.

©2012 by Thomas A. Jopling
All rights reserved.
No part of this book may be reproduced, or transmitted in any form, or by any method, electronic or mechanical, without written permission from the author.

Thomas A. Jopling
120 Saddlebrook Way
Alvaton, KY 42122

ISBN-13: 978-0615590042 (Disciplers)
ISBN-10: 0615590047

Printed in the USA by

DISCIPLERS Press

TABLE OF CONTENTS

7 *Introduction*
    GOD CAN USE ANYTHING, EVEN CHERRY LIP GLOSS

13 *Chapter One*
    AN UNLIKELY MISSIONARY

15 *Chapter Two*
    "YOU'RE CRAZY!"

23 *Chapter Three*
    LANGUAGE SCHOOL AND THE LESSON OF THE PEPPER

29 *Chapter Four*
    "SO, THIS IS HOME?"

33 *Chapter Five*
    ASSURANCE

35 *Chapter Six*
    STARTING A NEW MISSION

37 *Chapter Seven*
    EVERYDAY LIFE

39 *Chapter Eight*
    JOSÉ

41 *Chapter Nine*
    CLINIC WORK

43 *Chapter Ten*
    THE BIG GRINGO

45 *Chapter Eleven*
    FURLOUGH

TABLE OF CONTENTS
continued

47 Chapter Twelve
  ARMY DUTY

61 Chapter Thirteen
  A FUNERAL, A NEW BIRTH, AND A COUPLE OF WEDDINGS

65 Chapter Fourteen
  THEY CAME BY TWOS AND THREES

67 Chapter Fifteen
  A DAY WITH NOÉ

71 Chapter Sixteen
  CHURCH PLANTING: CARIBBEAN STYLE

75 Chapter Seventeen
  EARTHQUAKE!

79 Chapter Eighteen
  HIKING WITH HERMAN

83 Chapter Nineteen
  A NEW WATCHMAN

85 Chapter Twenty
  THE BULLET THAT BROUGHT LIFE

89 Epilogue
  THE HARDEST TIMES IN A MISSIONARY'S LIFE

For my amazing wife,
Valerie,
and for all those who choose to serve
HIM

Introduction

GOD CAN USE ANYTHING, EVEN CHERRY LIP GLOSS

I was born to a very humble family in rural southern Arkansas. My and my brother's nurturing was the group effort of our parents and both sets of grandparents. It was from life on the small family farm, in the pine forest hills and hardwood bottoms, and on the numerous nearby lakes and rivers that we developed our basic life skills. My grandparents were tireless in their efforts to instill the ethos of hard work, being a good neighbor, and respect for the natural world within me and they were very successful. And, as part of those lessons, there was the occasional Sunday morning trip to the local church's worship service. However, other than for this disassociated and rare visit to the church up the road and the five days of Vacation Bible School each summer that my aunt dutifully mandated for me, there really was no mention of God, church, Bible, salvation, heaven, hell, or any of those other church words in the conversations that my ears were privy to. That is except for a couple of funerals that I went to and even then I was more intrigued with the free cokes in the funeral home's refrigerator and visiting with my cousins than the idea of what happened to you after you died. And so, I pretty much lived in blissful ignorance of God until July of 1976.

It was on Saturday, the third of July that these two girls – good-looking girls, no, make that very good-looking girls – stepped off this white school bus that had the words "Stephens First Baptist Church" painted in blue letters on the side. This bus had seen better days and its loud sputtering had caught my and my brother's attention when it stopped at the head of our gravel drive. Well, we went out to meet these young ladies. Mary Helen and Sharon introduced themselves and told us that they were members of the First Baptist Church of the town that was some nineteen miles up the highway from our home. The church had recently decided to start a bus ministry, whatever that was, and these two young ladies wanted to know if my brother and I would be interested in riding to church on that bus with them tomorrow morning. Now, what do you think my answer was? I did not even think of getting permission from the folks. My fifteen year-old body had recently *god can use anything, even cherry lip gloss*

IT HELPS TO BE CRAZY!

jerked its hormone producing apparatus into high gear, which in turn had caused its thinking machine to come to nearly a complete stop.

Anyway, the next morning I had a great hour-long ride to church. I sat in a Sunday School class and sat through a church service. And it was the nation's bicentennial so we also had hamburgers and hot dogs and games that afternoon. Though this was my first visit to a church since I had become too old for my aunt's beginners class in VBS, I really was not that impressed with what went on. After all I was fifteen, knew it all, and had to be cool. (However, I was impressed with Mary Helen's lip gloss.) But when the youth leader told us that the coming weekend the church would be sponsoring a youth retreat at the Beech Springs church camp and that all of us were invited, my attention was peaked! Friday night, all day Saturday, and Saturday night in the presence of cherry lip gloss and Mary Helen and her sixteen year-old lips – YES!! Again, as you can already deduce, my motives for attending this evangelical outreach event to bring lost sinners into the family of the Mighty, Gracious, Forgiving God through the repentance of their evil, immoral sins of the flesh and their inviting the Lord and Savior, Jesus Christ, who died on that bloody cross on Calvary, into their broken hearts were not based upon a personal concern of whether my immortal spirit would dwell in the New Jerusalem or suffer in the fiery pit of Hades. (I did not say that I did not listen. I said that I was not that impressed.) Rather, this coming weekend sounded like fun and might lead to some quiet time with Glossy Lips. At least, that was what I was thinking when I put my name on the sign-up list and was what I dwelled upon for the next the five days.

Friday afternoon finally came around. The sputtering, white bus stopped at the head of the drive and I began the weekend of my dreams. The afternoon was good. The evening was better. Mary Helen and I were becoming friendly and she seemed like she was paying more attention to me than she was to the other guys. Things were looking good. Long about ten o'clock Danny-the-youth-leader yelled that it was time for the campfire devotional. Mary Helen and I found a log and rolled it up in to the growing circle of teenagers. She sat next to me. We looked at each other. I don't know what she saw in my eyes, but I know what was there. It was the reflection of the fire on cherry lip gloss. She smiled, leaned over to me, and she breathed warmly into my ear saying, "I really want you to listen to Danny. I think he's gonna say something that you really need to hear." I smiled. I nodded. I drooled just a bit. All I could do was blubber, "Okay" as I hoped that Mary Helen would think of something else that she needed to whisper to me. I really liked the smell of cherries.

god can use anything, even cherry lip gloss

IT HELPS TO BE CRAZY!

Mary Helen was right. I did hear some things that night that I needed to hear. They were things that started me to think about my future, a death that could come at any moment, and what happens after that death. While some of the things were things that I had heard the Sunday before, Danny had a way of saying those things, a way of explaining them, that made all those things personal. Sleep that night was long in coming. My mind would not shut down.

The next day, Saturday, July 10, 1976, was a long day. The games and activities were great fun, but I could not get Danny's words out of my mind. The next evening came and so did the campfire and devotional. But this time after telling a story of how one of his friends had died in a car wreck a few months earlier and how this friend had told Danny that he had plenty of time to get saved as he was only nineteen, Danny asked if there was anyone in our group who needed to be saved. I stood up. Danny took me to a nearby picnic table. There I found Christ waiting for me.

A week later, in the Sunday morning service, I was baptized. My maternal grandparents were there. And though this was the first time in several years that they had attended a church service, after this day, they very rarely missed a Sunday for the rest of their lives.

My parents were not there that day.

The rest of the summer and the following year was a paradox. I had a great time with my new friends as I learned more about God and about myself. But this new way of defining right and wrong, of describing selfishness and selflessness, caused me to look at my family and our lives in a different light. Over the next couple of years, my eyes became open to what was happening around me. It was also during this time that I was forced to grow up very quickly. I had to be responsible for myself completely. My room in my parent's home was mostly just a place to keep my clothes and to sleep a couple of nights a week. I almost never saw my parents; and when I did, I usually wished that I had not.

It was late August, 1978. My senior year of school had just begun. My father wanted to see me. We went out into the yard. He said that it was time for me to decide if I would join him in the business or not. If not, then it was time to go. I knew the business was not for me. I could not undertake a life in the criminal underworld. I had to leave. I had to break all ties – completely. My first thoughts, after the hurt and anger had subsided, were of Tim and his parents. Tim was my best friend. His parents were great people. Perhaps they could help me out. I was now attending a high school in a town 25 miles from my parent's home. Tim and his parent's lived in that town. Maybe they could take me in, or at least let me sleep there occasionally.

Tim's parents did take me in. Clerry and Glenda adopted a new son, me! They loved me, they disciplined me, they took care of me, and they worried about me. They even got mad at me and yelled at me! They truly became my parents in every way. And I corrupted their younger son just like an older brother is supposed to do. They were also the best example of God that anyone could hope to find on this planet. It was in them that I saw a bit of Jesus and it was in them that I found a Christian example that I wanted to follow. It was while I was hugging Clerry's and Glenda's neck the night of my high school graduation that I swore that I would do my best to make them proud of me. They deserved it. They loved me when others did not. They were the picture of Jesus that I could see and touch.

And if you are wondering about Mary Helen, well, she discovered Larry during that summer of '76. Larry was my friend who drove an orange '71 Plymouth Road Runner. It had a flames detail paint job. I drove a rusted '65 Ford Ranchero. His dream was to live a life of fast driving, excitement, and danger. My dream was to be a philosopher. I guess the bad boy persona was more intriguing than the Socrates one. One day the following summer Larry left in a spray of gravel and a cloud of cannabis smoke. I never heard what happened to Larry. I ended up teaching philosophy and theology and living more experiences in one lifetime than I ever thought possible.

Tom Jopling
Alvaton, Kentucky
January, 2012

It Helps to be Crazy!

chapter one

AN UNLIKELY MISSIONARY

Most people have their own ideas of what type of person becomes a missionary. And if you would have asked, just about anyone who knew me before my thirtieth birthday would have quickly told you that I was an unlikely candidate to ever be a missionary.

I was not brought up in a home in which God, church, or serving others was emphasized. Church attendance was a rare thing. The word missionary, to my recollection, was never even uttered by anyone in my family.

Even after I became a believer and a church goer, and even later after I had begun to serve in the local church, the idea or thought of being a missionary or doing mission work never crossed my mind. I thought missionaries were super Christians, who had memorized the entire Bible before graduating from seminary, oozed holiness from their pores rather than sweat, had never listened to rock music or uttered a four-letter word, and had been specially created without that inherent, sinful nature that mere mortals, like me, had been born with. Therefore, you can probably understand why I was so confused when I realized that God was calling me to the mission field. Not that I ever doubted that calling, but I was puzzled that He would call me, someone who did not in any way fit what I thought was the criteria for a missionary. It was all I could do to recite John 3:16 and "Jesus wept". (Still can't remember the address for that verse.) I was a product of the 70s and I owned albums by the rock groups Kiss and Queen. And there were very few minutes in a day that passed in which I did not sin or think about doing a sinful act. Even my dreams, for the most part, were unspeakable outside an army barracks or the men's shower room at We are Filthy Rags University.

However, God introduced me to one of His great men, Brother Earl. Brother Earl was a retired pastor and missionary. Brother Earl was also a real person and not one of those super Christians that I thought were the only ones that were qualified to play on God's mission team. Brother Earl taught me that God calls those whom He has prepared, is preparing, and will prepare and that this calling is not limited to our past or even to our present abilities. He said that God calls us because He knows what our future capabilities can be and how those capabilities are going to fit into His future work. Brother Earl said that God calls those who have made themselves available to be called.

That was when it began to make sense to me. God calls people to do His work based not upon past or present performance but based upon our future performance. He already knows what that performance can be. We just have to choose to do it.

So my past performance was horrible. My present performance was lacking in every category. But I must have a future that looks promising to God. If He feels that this most unlikely candidate to be missionary can do the job, then who am I to argue.

IT HELPS TO BE CRAZY!

chapter two

"YOU'RE CRAZY!"

The two words, "you're crazy", have probably been used to describe me more often than any other words. When I was in high school they flowed from the lips of many young ladies of whose company I sought for a Friday night. I heard them from other trainees in boot camp as I zealously engaged them in mock combat. I have also heard them from my fellow firefighters and paramedics just before or right after I committed some ill-advised act that I thought was necessary to do a job that needed to be done. I have heard them from close friends and total strangers. And, perhaps, they are all correct. I have always done those things that most people would not do for whatever reason. But that's okay. The way I see things, it is those who do the things that others will not do that keep the world moving along. I also truly believe that God will and can use the crazies of this world to accomplish His will. Most of the missionaries that I know have been called crazy. After all, the words of Christ tell us that just being a Christian will make us appear strange to the rest of the world. And I believe being a missionary requires a little bit of daring, a little stubbornness, and a considerable amount of craziness. Even if craziness isn't necessary to being happy in your life's current station, you have to admit that being a little crazy is still a good way to get things done. People will look at you a little strangely, but then they usually just get out of your way, allowing you to pretty much do what you need to do without them telling you that you can't do it that way. Being a little crazy does have its advantages.

It was August 8, 1990. I was a firefighter/paramedic with the Springdale Arkansas Fire Department. I was very happy. I had been with the department for five years and I was progressing up the rank structure and about to test for Lieutenant. Life was good in the home. I was very active in our church and was very attentive to God. I was literally soaking up every word that I heard or read that pertained to God, Jesus, or the Bible. However, every time I heard a sermon I started preaching it in my mind along with the preacher. I started adding things to the sermon. On the way back home I would question aloud, much to my wife's chagrin, "Why didn't he say..." or

IT HELPS TO BE CRAZY!

"Why did his points not include..." I knew that I could preach those sermons. I wanted to preach those sermons. I also begin to have a huge burden for lost souls. I wanted to lead people to the Lord. It became almost an obsession.

That Sunday night, my daughter, Dalaina, was to be baptized. We had led her to the Lord the week before and this was her special night. But there was something else there, in my heart, in my soul, in my mind. When my pastor started saying words about serving God and being willing to do whatever it was He wanted from us, I knew he was preaching to me. I called my wife, Valerie, outside.

"Val, God wants me to be a preacher. I have to surrender to His call."

She looked me dead in the eye, smiled sweetly, and said, "You're crazy!" She then went back inside, leaving me to wrestle with God on my own. She wasn't being mean. She just trusted me to do the right thing without her blurring up the situation and commingling my thoughts with her wishes and ideas.

During the invitation I walked the isle, tears falling on the carpet the whole trip. I could hardly speak the words to my pastor and the church. On the spot, they licensed me to preach. I later found out from our pastor and other members, from other preachers and friends, and from Valerie, that they all knew that I had been called to preach long before I did. Such is the way of God. Sometimes the one called is the last to know or to realize that he or she is being called.

It was also that night that I received my first inclination that we would be missionaries someday. One of Valerie's best friends, Jan, as she came to hug my neck said to me in a very serious tone, "Don't you go and take Valerie to the jungle as some missionary." Her words touched something in my mind. "Missionary," I thought. "Hmmm." Isn't it funny how God will give us hints about our future and prepare us for His work when we really have no idea what is going on?

About three months later I attended the Baptist Missionary Association of America (BMAA) Mission Symposium in Dallas, Texas. It was three days of hearing from different missionaries about how God was working around the world. My heart was touched from the first words of the first speaker through to the end of the symposium. During the last sermon a challenge was given to those men and women who might be listening and felt that God might be dealing with them. I fell into that category. The speaker said to surrender to God. God can and will take care of the details. During the invitation I walked the aisle and told God that if He wanted me to be a missionary that I would go wherever He wanted me to go and do whatever He wanted me to

IT HELPS TO BE CRAZY!

do. I then took then Director of Foreign Missions of the BMAA, Jerry Kidd, by the hand and told him that God wanted me to be a missionary someday. Director Kidd smiled and said a few words like, "Bless you," and, "Allow God to work with you." He was not being rude or disrespectful. You have to understand that there were at least twenty other young men and women who had said the same thing to him during this meeting. It had been a great meeting, full of God, good reports, and emotions. And the director knew that young people, like me, would often get caught up in the emotion of a moment. It was also the first time that Director Kidd had ever seen me. I was just some young man crying his eyes out and saying words that he hears hundreds of times a year.

When I arrived home the next day I told Valerie that we were going to be missionaries. Guess what she said. You're right. She said, "You're crazy!"

Though God had been using me every Sunday in a pulpit somewhere, she knew I still lacked a lot and that I was no way near ready to do something like this. Plus, at that time, she had no desire to leave the land of Wal-Mart.

Over the next couple of years I continuously prayed about and thought about where and how we might serve as missionaries. Valerie prayed that I would listen to God and not to Tom. I had also begun formal Bible courses through Central Baptist College during that time. And God continued to allow me to preach. Every week I filled pulpits. During those years before my first pastorate and ordination I preached more than most pastors. I prayed every day that God would give me somewhere to preach and He honored my prayers. I also had the opportunity to lead several people to Christ. I was snake-bit. I loved seeing lost souls saved.

Sometime in 1992, I (major emphasis on "*I*") figured out that we were supposed to go to Papua New Guinea as missionaries. I went to the library and learned all I could about that country. I also began to teach myself Pidgin English. This went on until a pastor friend of mine set up a meeting for me with then BMAA missionary to Honduras, Charles Spurgeon. Charles was in the States on furlough.

Charles Spurgeon had been on the field for a number of years. He was a dentist as well as a church planter. He had a clinic in the mountains of Honduras and wanted to expand into a general medicine. He thought with my medical background that I could be of assistance in the clinic. We agreed that I would accompany him to Honduras in April of '93 for an eight-day stay.

April arrived and I made my first trip out of the USA. Wow, were my eyes opened to world politics. We landed at three different Central American airports along the way. At each of them I saw anti-aircraft guns along the *you're crazy!*

IT HELPS TO BE CRAZY!

runways, tanks guarding the terminals, and fighter aircraft on the tarmacs. There were soldiers everywhere and they all had machine-guns. I began to wonder if this was where I wanted to bring my wife and children.

We arrived in Honduras and were met by another BMAA missionary, Bobby Bowman. He took us to his home, which was about a two-hour drive from the airport. The drive was along a road that was supposed to be asphalt but had little evidence of ever having been topped with asphalt. We had to ford several creeks and a couple of rivers along the way as most of the bridges were either completely gone or almost gone. And did I ever experience culture shock! There were people begging for food along the streets. I saw kids holding up iguanas for sale. There were as many ox carts on the roads as automobiles. And women were breast-feeding their babies right there in public for all to see. The public bathrooms were wherever you happened to be standing when the urge hit you. The houses were made from adobe and thatch and sometimes from cardboard, paper and plastic garbage bags. My eyes were opened to a world that had only previously existed on those 'save the children' commercials and in National Geographic magazines and TV specials.

After a short visit in the Bowman's home, Charles and I took off to the mountain town of Santa Rosa de Copán. It was another two and a half-hour drive. The further we went into the mountains the worse the road became. We had to dodge rockslides, cattle, chickens, ox-carts, burros, buses, and people. It seemed that the national pastime was to congregate on the road, lie down, and see just how close the cars would come to you before you rolled out of the way.

It was when we stopped in a village to buy a coke that God again touched my heart. As I stood at the counter, drinking my coke and eating a stale Butterfinger, a girl, about six years-old, dirty, malnourished, wearing tattered clothing stood watching me. I had eaten about half of the candy bar when I gave her the rest. I figured she would just gobble it down. However, she walked over to her mother, who was sitting about ten yards away holding a younger girl, a sister I presumed. This girl then broke that half of a Butterfinger bar into three parts and shared it with her mother and sister. Another example of how God uses the meek in His world. It was this moment that I began to realize that this was the place where God wanted me serve Him.

The next day I was exposed face to face with the people of Honduras and a love for them began to grow within my heart. That night I attended a service in the mission in Santa Rosa. I did not need to understand the

IT HELPS TO BE CRAZY!

conversation around me to feel the Holy Spirit's presence and His dealing with me. The hymn, *At the Cross*, when they sang it, just broke my heart. By the end of the second day I was close to being sure that this country was going to be my future home.

My third day in Honduras we went even deeper into the mountains. We went to a small village named Santa Rosita. It was a two-hour trip along horrible mountain roads. The village was poor even by Honduran standards. No electricity, no running water, no businesses; nothing but dust, rocks, farm animals running wild, and people. We had a service in the schoolyard that night by the light of a lantern. Fifty or so people, a bunch of chickens, two goats, a mule, three hogs, and a burro were present. The songs were upbeat, the conversation lively, and although I could not understand the preaching, there were a lot of "amens". The kids just stared at me and all the adults had to shake my hand and talk to me. Once again the Spirit touched me and by the time we were heading back to Santa Rosa there was not a doubt in my mind or heart. Honduras was the place.

The next five days were filled with experiences. I took about 200 photographs during those days. I wanted to record every sight and experience to take home and share with Valerie and the others. When we left Honduras headed back to the States I cried. The love that had grown inside me for the people and the country of Honduras had changed. It now was not only a love, but also a burden. I wanted to go back to Honduras and help those people to find Christ as their personal Savior.

Valerie met me at the airport. After we exchanged hugs and kisses she asked me how the trip was. I said, "Val, we are going to move to Honduras."

Once again I heard those words, "You're crazy!"

Over the next couple of months I tried to relate to her and the older children about my experiences. I also started checking into a few different mission organizations and praying that God would open the doors for us to become missionaries in Honduras if that was His will. The first organization that I contacted was the BMAA. I was unofficially told that the BMAA prefers their missionaries to have some college or seminary level Bible study as well as some pastoral experience. I continued my studies through CBC and started praying that God would take care of the pastoral experience. I also continued my work as a firefighter/paramedic and began to read every type of book on general medicine that I could find.

Two months later in June of '93, Springdale Missionary Baptist Church asked me to serve as their associate pastor and I served in that role for about a month. In early August, Old Baptist Mission in Westville, Oklahoma called me to serve as their pastor. I let them know up front that I was certain that sometime in the future that I would be a missionary and that we were pursuing that calling as God led. They accepted this news and still felt I was to be their pastor. I accepted their call to be their pastor, was ordained, and served there for the next two years.

In April of 1994, Valerie accompanied me back to Honduras. She was often a little quicker about spiritual things than I was. This was one of those times. The night we arrived in country we visited a small village named Portrerillos. This village was very similar to the village of Santa Rosita that I had visited the year before. She cried during the service; fell in love with the people and that love changed to a burden all before the end of the preaching. She told me that night as we laid down, "Yes Tom, we are supposed to be here."

When we returned to the States, our preparations to follow God's calling to the mission field intensified. We started preparing friends and relatives and the children. We made formal application with the BMAA in July. I completed a few more Bible courses and I began an internship with a couple of family doctors. I intensified my reading on general medicine. And we prayed. We asked for God's guidance and that He would open the doors. I also learned patience. In August, we met with the Directors of the BMAA Mission Department. Director Jerry Kidd knew who I was now. The meeting was positive. Valerie and I explained to them what we felt God would have us to do in Honduras. We wanted to be church planters and use children's nutrition programs and a limited medical program as door openers and as a way to physically help the people there. We wanted to work in the Santa Rosa area. We also learned, quite unexpectedly, that Charles Spurgeon had left the field and that we would be on our own.

We met with the Missionary Advisory Committee of the BMAA in November. They asked us many questions and they asked about our call to be missionaries in Honduras. The best that I could manage between the tears was that I was homesick to get back to Honduras. The next day we were told that we would be recommended to the BMAA body of churches the following April at the national meeting.

The next four months was the longest period of my life. I really learned patience during this time. I continued as pastor of Old Baptist Mission; however, my heart was in Honduras.

April 1995 arrived and Valerie, the two oldest children, and I made the trip to Dallas. Here I was, back again in that city where God had first touched my heart for missions five years earlier. Our family was a lot larger this time.

IT HELPS TO BE CRAZY!

We now had five children. Joshua was 14, Dalaina 11, Melanie 4, Joel 3, and Danielle was four months old. We enjoyed the services and the sessions of the meeting. The preaching was great, the singing beautiful, but it was that last business session that we were so anxious for. That was when the business of the Missions Department and the sending of missionaries were to be handled. The recommendations from the Advisory Committee were read and that was when I quit breathing. There were several minutes of discussion regarding other missionaries, money matters, and other things like that. I don't believe I had ever been so nervous in my whole life except for my wedding day, and this day was going to be as equally life changing. The moderator finally got around to calling for a vote of those in favor of Tom Jopling serving as a missionary in Honduras, Central America. There was not any opposition. We were going! Valerie and I hugged, cried, and made complete idiots of ourselves there on the back row of that auditorium.

A few minutes later all of the new missionaries with their families and all the veteran missionaries that were present were brought up on stage. There we were, the Joplings, standing before several thousand people representing some 1300 churches and we were missionaries. I will never forget it. They prayed for us all, took pictures, and hugged us and shook our hands. *I was now a missionary!* I always knew that the title *missionary* would carry a lot of responsibility, but I didn't know just how much until we were leaving the auditorium. A distinguished looking gentleman whom I had never seen before walked up to me and grasped my hand, told me what church he was from, said that he would be praying for me and then walked away leaving a $100 bill in my hand. That was when it really hit me. There were now literally thousands of believers praying for me, and giving of their money to support my family and me as we represented them and God as their missionaries. The tears started again.

We began deputation May 1, 1995 and for a little over three months we visited churches all over the central part of the U.S. We traveled from New Orleans to Illinois, from western Oklahoma to Eastern Mississippi. The people were very receptive to us everywhere we visited. I remember some churches that we visited said we were the first missionaries to ever visit them. A couple of the churches did not know who or what the BMAA was. To a couple of them it was just some initials on their sign. All in all it was a good time for us. We made new friends, and we educated a few people about the BMAA and their missionaries during this time, also.

We also said our good-byes during these three months. We were the guests of honors at several going away parties and family gatherings. Of course, there were a lot of tears but we were ready to start our new lives in Central America and that softened the heartaches.

On the morning of August 14, 1995, family, friends, and the mission directors saw us off from the Little Rock airport as we left for Central America. A new chapter in the lives of the Jopling family was about to begin.

chapter three

LANGUAGE SCHOOL
AND THE LESSON OF THE PEPPER

We were on our way. We were all excited. Valerie and I were also a little apprehensive about taking the five children into a part of the world that some people still referred to as uncivilized. Joshua and Dalaina were ready to see all of the things that Valerie and I had described to them over the past couple of years. Melanie wanted to make new friends. Joel was ready to see a jaguar in real life, which he told to any and every one whom he happened to see on the plane. Danielle wanted to pull the gold wings off of the stewardess's blouse. Our first home in Central America was to be the city of San Jose, Costa Rica. There we would live and study the Spanish language for a year and to learn the Latin culture. Valerie and I did not know any Spanish except for a couple of important words: *comida* and *servicio*, which mean food and bathroom respectively. And with Costa Rica having the highest economic level and most industrialized of the Central American countries, it would be a good place for us North Americans to get over our Wal-Mart withdrawals.

We met up with two other newly elected BMAA missionary families on our flight south. John Calloway and his new wife Melanie, who would be going on to Bolivia after language school, and Randy and Kristen Scaggs, who would head on to the Dominican Republic after Costa Rica. During the coming year we all would become close friends.

Our year in Costa Rica would be an adventure, and it started out with a bang. As we flew over Central America we encountered some storms. We were advised that due to the weather conditions we would be detouring into Panama City, Panama for the night instead of San Jose. That made us just a little nervous because there was no one to meet us to help us find the necessary things that we might need, like food, water, and bathrooms. Joel started to cry because he was not going to Costa Rica and he would not see his jaguar. We finally landed about 10pm. The airline had arranged for buses to take the whole flight to a hotel for the night. However, there were more passengers than seats and so the Jopling family had to wait for a taxi. Finally

language school and the lesson of the pepper

IT HELPS TO BE CRAZY!

the airline found a taxi that was big enough for our carry-on luggage and us. It was an old Chevrolet station wagon that appeared to have seen service in World War II as a tank and had taken plenty of punishment. I had to hold the front passenger door closed as we went down the road. As we rounded the corners a very loud high-pitched scream that made any nearby dog howl radiated from the front end. We hit one bump in the road and the rear view mirror fell into my lap. The driver was much like the vehicle itself. He was both blind and deaf or he truly desired to commit suicide and to take us with him. We were doing 60 mph down city streets weaving in between other taxis, vehicles, trashcans, drunks, bicycles, lovers holding hands, and dodging any smooth places in the street. The only things he did not weave between were the potholes. It seemed that he went out of his way to find every bump and hole in the road. And did you know that in Panama a yellow traffic light is the signal to punch the accelerator, stick your head out the open window, and to yell and spit loudly at any object or person that might be in the area of the intersection?

We finally arrived at a very nice hotel about midnight. We were told to be ready to leave from the lobby at 5 a.m. After a few hours of fitful sleep, we made our way down to the lobby. We were bused back to the airport. About 8 a.m., after two and a half hours of sitting in the airport trying to keep Joel and Melanie from destroying the terminal and creating an international incident that would have all of us serving lifetime imprisonment in a Panama jail cell, the flight crew made their way on board. We took off about thirty minutes later. Joel, once again, told everyone on board that he was going to Costa Rica and would get to see a jaguar.

About a half-hour later we arrived at the San Jose airport. We got off the plane and headed towards customs. As we did so, Joel let all the security people know that he was now in Costa Rica and wanted to see a jaguar. I was dreading the customs check because we had 21 footlockers full of everything we needed to set up housekeeping for the coming year. I just knew they were going to have us unlock everything and then we would have to pay some huge tax for those 15-year-old pots and pans. I began praying about the time I got in line. Ten minutes later when it was our turn to stand before the inspector, either Valerie or God pinched Danielle. (I still don't know which.) Danielle began to wail and cry so loudly that the jets taking off were drowned out. After checking just one piece of our luggage the inspector, with one hand covering one ear, stamped our paper and waved us all through. Another prayer answered.

language school and the lesson of the pepper

IT HELPS TO BE CRAZY!

BMAA missionaries Dennis Murr and Phil Knott who were serving in Costa Rica met us there. They took all three travel weary, new missionary families to what would be their homes for the coming year. It turned out that we were to have a nice, big house only a few blocks from our language school and about a 20-minute walk from the kid's school. Our home was within a short walk of four different language schools, so the area markets and businesses were used to gringos (North Americans) that could not speak Spanish. Thus we began our year of language study and of becoming acquainted with the Latin culture.

Dennis and Phil wanted us to get in the missionary frame of mind right off so it was only after a couple of weeks that Phil invited the three new guys out to a building project in a small village a couple of hours away. After working hard one Saturday morning, the local pastor's wife prepared lunch for us: beans and rice with lemonade. There was also a jar of brownish, clear liquid with a roundish, red pepper in it. The pastor poured a little of the liquid onto his beans and then handed the jar to me. Being an old southern boy, I grew up with hot peppers to go along with beans so I just poured a little of the juice over my beans and then forked what I thought was the last pepper in what had been a jar of many peppers. After a couple of bites of beans and rice I, picked up this juicy pepper and took a healthy bite of it. Approximately two seconds later I opened my mouth and great tongues of fire shot forth out if it... and it was not the Holy Spirit! THAT LITTLE ROUND PEPPER WAS PURE FIRE! I made a few sounds that must have resembled those of evil spirits as everyone at the table turned to look at me with bewildered and shocked expressions. I then reached for the glass of lemonade in front of me and attempted to extinguish the raging fire in my mouth. Not enough in the glass! As I was reaching for the pitcher to refill my glass, Phil and the others realized what I done and began to laugh at my agonizing death right before their eyes. The national pastor was either serious or a very good actor. He was looking very aggravated and started throwing his hands into the air and speaking in rapid Spanish. Phil just laughed harder and translated the pastor's words for us, "I can't believe you did that! You ate THE PEPPER! Now I have to go all the way to Panama and get another one." It turned out that this was a Panamanian Savina Roja Habanero. One of these small bundles of pure fire is potent enough to launch the Space Shuttle into a low orbit around the Earth or to create several quarts of pepper sauce when placed in vinegar, tomatoes, or any other blended vegetable. You are not supposed to ever eat the pepper by itself because it is one of the hottest peppers known to man. However, this mere mortal had done so. Everyone had a good laugh while I stood around

language school and the lesson of the pepper
IT HELPS TO BE CRAZY!

the water faucet. About six hours later, after going through three quarts of lemonade, a gallon of water, and a quart of milk I started to have a little relief. I reflected on this important lesson I had learned of living in a foreign country. Never put anything into your mouth until you see someone else doing so, and then only do so with great caution.

A couple of months after the pepper experience, the three new missionary families decided that we were up to doing a little sightseeing on our own. We took a group tour to see one of the most active volcanoes in the world. It was a magnificent sight as lava, smoke, ash, and fire shot out of this perfect cone. Just like a National Geographic magazine cover. There were also some hot springs located near the volcano that had been turned into a small swimming area and observation area. Being an avid hiker I decided to do some exploring in the surrounding jungle with a couple of other students. About a mile into the jungle I felt something pop in my right calf muscle and my right foot ceased to work. The pain seemed to ease a bit after a couple of minutes and I was able to hobble back to the main group. By the time I made it back to the swim area, my leg had already begun to swell significantly and the pain was increasing. I knew I had a problem. However, this was a Saturday afternoon and the closest medical facility was several hours away and there were no more buses headed back into town that night. I would have to tough it out till the next day. By the time I got to a hospital Sunday night about nine o'clock, my leg was twice its normal size and my foot was blue and cold. I had torn the calf muscle and the swelling had cut off circulation to the foot. It was not a good situation. A surgeon was called in and preparations were made to cut into the leg to relieve the pressure before I lost my foot. He decided to wait another hour. He came back and said we will wait another hour. This went on for twelve hours. Between his visits I was really getting close to God and begging that God's will be done but also telling God that I really did not want to lose my foot or to have surgery. The swelling finally started to go down a little. I was in the hospital for four days and on crutches for a couple of weeks. It took over a year before I ever regained full strength in that leg. Another lesson to remember, 911 does not exist everywhere and a small accident can sometimes have major repercussions.

There are also many good memories of our time in Costa Rica. The language school was excellent and the instructors were beautiful people. The school specialized in training missionaries. All of the teachers were born again Christians. A couple of them were deacons and one was a Baptist pastor. The classes were small. The school also admitted a few non-missionary students to round out the classes. In my class were Randy, John, myself, and a young lady from Taiwan. She was very soft spoken and sweet. She was also Buddhist. Our pronunciation teacher was the Baptist pastor and the four of us all had a great desire that this young lady would find Christ before she left the school. Several months into school one of our lessons was to go through the plan of salvation in Spanish with a partner. Mae, the young Taiwanese lady was my partner. I went through the whole plan and as I was nearing the end of my presentation I asked the question, "Would you like to pray to Jesus at this time for salvation?" To my surprise, Mae said yes. I looked kind of dumfounded and asked if she was serious or if she was just playing the part. She said that she wanted to be a Christian. Well I was quite excited at this point. We had been praying for her for several months and trying to be good witnesses to her and here was the harvest. I asked for my teacher to assist me with this part because my Spanish was still very weak and this was too serious a time to be stumbling over words. My first opportunity to lead someone to Jesus in the Spanish language and she was Chinese. Try to tell me that there is no God in control... bringing a poor south Arkansas boy to a Spanish language school in Central America to witness to the daughter of a very rich Taiwanese family in a language that was new to both of us. Yes, God has His ways.

After a year of language school we were ready to move on. One year to the day after arriving in Costa Rica, we left that beautiful country for the United States. There we would make final arrangements and prepare our furniture and household things for shipping to Honduras, the country that God had called us to as our adopted home and place of service.

IT HELPS TO BE CRAZY!

chapter four

"SO, THIS IS HOME?"

After six days in the States in which we packed up most of our earthly possessions into a seagoing container, Joshua and I hopped a plane and headed for Honduras. We were planning on arriving before the rest of the family in order to get the house prepared and to make the transition from the land of Wal-Mart to the land of "What's a mall?" a little easier. Joshua realized pretty quickly that we were no longer in Arkansas when we dodged a seven-foot boa constrictor that was in the road not too many kilometers from the airport.

And speaking of the house, now here is another example of how God answers prayers in big ways. Valerie and I had been praying for the house situation the whole year we had been in Costa Rica. We both knew what most houses were like in Honduras, so we both had a few fears. For instance, finding a house big enough for a family of seven gringos that had not been recently used as a cattle barn was not going to be easy. And we each had our personal prayer request for the house. I would pray nightly, "God you know how much water this family uses. You know we have to have our baths and think of all those dirty clothes that have to be washed. Now God, I know that water is a very precious commodity in Honduras, but God could you help us out with the water situation and at least provide a good spring near the house?" And Valerie's prayer went something like, "Okay, God, we know that no house in Honduras has a yard larger than door mat, and in fact there is not even a word for "yard" in their vocabulary. But, Lord, we have a Joel. And if I am going to survive in that country you know that we have to have a place for Joel to get outside during the day." Well, we left things is God's hands. After all, he knows the real estate market better than we do. God also used our house-hunting to remind us that His timing is certainly not ours. It was the last day of our stay in Costa Rica, and despite our diligent prayers and activities, we had still not heard anything positive on our Honduras house search. That afternoon the telephone rang. It was the national pastor in Santa Rosa. He had heard of a possible house that he had not yet seen but wanted to know if he could reserve it if it seemed suitable. I gleefully said yes.

"so, this is home?"

IT HELPS TO BE CRAZY!

By that point in time, we would take anything and worry about comfort, critters, and solid walls later.

Well, when Joshua and I drove up to the house, I simply began to bless God! He had found us something that I did not even know existed. The house that he provided for us was unbelievable. It turned out to be one of the largest homes in western Honduras; a four bedroom, two bath, ranch style home. It even had an inside kitchen with running water. No hot water, but, hey. And the water system...two deep wells and a cistern so large that you could park four pickup trucks in it. We had more water than the rest of the country put together. And the yard... two acres of the most beautiful grass you have ever seen with several kinds of fruit and shade trees. The place looked like a park. I guess that it was God's way of letting us know that He does pay attention to the details of our prayers.

Over the next couple of weeks, Joshua and I worked to make the house into a home. We did a little painting, purchased a few pieces of furniture, and waited on the household shipment that was making its way from New Orleans on an empty banana boat. Finally, only thirteen days late, we received our shipment on the day before Valerie and the rest of the clan were to arrive. (Interestingly, we were told that we set a new record for getting the paperwork and the custom's inspection completed and getting the shipment delivered. Again God answered the prayer.) All that day and well into the night Joshua and I worked feverishly trying to get the house in somewhat of an order. As you can imagine, we did not succeed. The place was still a disaster area when we left the next morning for the airport.

The airport was something out an of old black and white movie. Hot, run down, full of mosquitoes, with about three thousand people all shouting to the top of their lungs. Somewhere in this mess were my wife and four younger children and twenty-five pieces of luggage. Finally I saw her, sweat pouring off her brow, hair in tangles, clothes sticking to her body. It was Valerie, my beautiful wife. She was standing at the customs table with an official who was pointing at the luggage and screaming something about start opening every piece for inspection and taxes. It was about that time that baby Danielle, whom Dalaina was holding, started to cry. Not just a normal cry, but a bellowing, ear-splitting, high-pitched yell. Valerie and Dalaina swear that they did not pinch the child, so maybe it was the Holy Spirit again. It didn't really matter who did the pinching but the crying child worked. The customs' agent covered her ears and motioned with her head for Valerie, the bellowing baby, the other three kids, and the twenty-five pieces of luggage to leave the building as quickly as possible. Again God answered prayers.

"so, this is home?"

IT HELPS TO BE CRAZY!

About five hours later we reached our new home in Santa Rosa. Valerie started crying as she got out of the truck and started looking around at how God had blessed us. Melanie and Joel immediately started looking for trees to climb and fruit to eat and began shouting, "This is a great place to live." Dalaina walked through the house and stated, "So this is home? What, no cable?"

chapter five

ASSURANCE

For the next three weeks we began to settle into our new home with our new neighbors and in this new culture. Let me tell you that there was nothing easy about this transformation; neither for us nor for our neighbors. We felt like the neighborhood goldfish with everyone looking at us. And they literally were. People would come and stand outside the front gate just watching and listening. Some of the bolder ones would actually walk up on the porch and look into the windows. At first we didn't know what they were planning, but it soon became obvious that they were just curious about this new, gringo family. Their culture shock to us was just as great as our culture shock to them.

During those first few weeks Valerie and I had asked God to make it plain to us that we had actually followed His will and that this wasn't just some hair-brained stunt that we were involved with. He gave us that assurance. The first two times that I preached in my horrible Spanish, professions of faith were made. The community and the people accepted us with open arms and really made us feel at home. We actually begin to feel more at home in this new land than we did the last three or four years that we were in the states. We felt permanence, something we had not felt in a long time.

Though we felt that we were to be church-planting missionaries, we realized that the existing two missions in our area of Honduras needed help and should be given top priority in our work effort. We immediately began visiting, preaching, teaching and offering any kind of assistance that we could to these missions, the pastors, and their members. God blessed those efforts. Within a few months, the mission at Cucuyagua was ready to organize into an independent church and to start a new mission. We purchased a building sitting on an acre of land, remodeled the building, cleaned up the land, and opened the Mt. Horeb Baptist Mission. The new church at Cucuyagua was now a multi-campus church! Within a year the mission had outgrown the mother church. Though I did a lot of the preaching and teaching during that first year, it was national missionary and pastor Manuel Pinto who did the real work in this this church. Manuel was a real example for me. The only *assurance*

IT HELPS TO BE CRAZY!

thing that kept him from doing more than he already did was the number of hours in the day. He pastored a church, a mission, and preached and taught in two other villages. Manual would preach three sermons in three different locations each Sunday and then preach and teach two or three other evenings during the week. I am honored to be associated with men like Manuel as these men are the real soldiers in God's army.

One morning as Joshua, national missionary Paco (Francisco Espinoza), and I were headed from Santa Rosa to the Cucuyagua area, we encountered an overturned truck on the mountain road. It was a large box truck and it was dangling precariously over the edge of the cliff. We also noticed that there were a lot of bystanders hanging around the broke open doors of the truck. As we approached to investigate what was going on people started grabbing up the new car batteries that had spilled out of the back of the truck. So these folks were doing a little looting. No big surprise. But what we saw next did surprise us. There, pinned in the cab of the truck was the driver. And no one was offering any assistance to him though he was yelling loudly for someone to help him. The people had decided that they either would not or could not help the driver, but they could help themselves to some new batteries. Seeing this situation, old instincts kicked in and I started shouting orders at Josh, at Paco, and at the surprised bystanders and looters. Someone had to help this guy and we didn't have Rescue 911 to call. We were it. I crawled into the cab and started doing what I could for his injuries while the other folks were gathering up chains, pry bars, hacksaws, and a mule harness with a mule. We used all of these items over the next hour as we worked to free the severely injured man. Finally, about the time the police and the ambulance arrived we had the man free. Though he had lost his truck, his cargo, and one leg, he still had his life.

Paco visited the man a couple of days later in the hospital and the man also found Christ. Another example of how God can use life's bystanders and precarious situations to bring about His will.

chapter six

STARTING A NEW MISSION

As I mentioned earlier, we did not immediately have plans to start a new mission in Santa Rosa. However, that is kind of what happened. You see, being from Arkansas it is just natural for us to be neighborly. And that is what we were, neighborly. Valerie and I would go over to our neighbors' houses and sit out on a rock or under a tree and just visit. Maybe drink a little coffee and just enjoy time with them. We did this every day and everywhere. And we soon noticed that there were a lot of kids around our house. So being in love with kids, we decided we would start doing something every week with the neighborhood kids. Not having any children's programs in Spanish, we looked to what we might have in English and could modify. The BMAA Sunbeam program looked promising.

Contacting the Casa Bautista Misionera de Publicaciones we found out that a missionary had previously translated the lesson plans of the program but not the visuals. After receiving a copy of the lesson plans we set out to modify and translate the visuals into Spanish using a desktop computer.

Shortly thereafter, we started having weekly Sunbeam meetings for the local kids. By the third week we had out grown our living room and had to move out to the porch. A month later we had to move out to the gazebo. We began to notice that not only did we have kids coming to the meetings, but adults also. Mothers, fathers, big brothers and sisters, and grandparents were coming to these classes. It was really something to see a little lady in her tortilla-making apron or a grizzled coffee bean picker with his old hat and machete coloring a picture of Noah and the Ark.

We noticed that people started making professions of faith during the meetings and during the week. Sometimes people would come and knock on our door and say, "Brother Tom, Sister Val, I want to get saved right now." We were reaching the people with the Gospel through a children's program!

After about nine months of this we had outgrown the gazebo, and we realized that we had planted a mission without even trying. This was great! God also worked it out that this was about the time that the older mission in *starting a new mission*

IT HELPS TO BE CRAZY!

Santa Rosa was mature enough to organize into a church. So now in Santa Rosa we had a church up town and a mission just out of town.

It was also during this time that I learned another important lesson in being a missionary: This being, NEVER ASK WHAT YOU ARE EATING. JUST SMILE AND ENJOY. One day I took a trip to the farm of one of our church members. It is a huge farm and is covered by Mayan ruins and artifacts. After a day of exploring these ruins and going inside the pyramids and seeing two thousand year old skeletons and other such sights, it was time for a good, hearty meal. We had beans, rice, tortillas and the best tasting pork roast I had ever eaten. Or at least I thought it was pork roast. As I was biting into my second helping of this meat, I was asked to pass the tongue. I must have looked kind of puzzled because the host repeated his request. This time I was sure of what I heard. "Please pass the beef tongue." The taste of that meat just changed right there in my mouth – kind of like magic.

So remember, eat heartily, smile, enjoy, and don't ask.

chapter seven

EVERYDAY LIFE

The next several months were basically uneventful. We had become well-adjusted and were enjoying our new lives as missionaries. Though the time was mostly uneventful there were some interesting times. I guess the best way to fill you in on some of the more interesting times is through the words of my diary.

November 6, 1996 – During the past week I worked with surgery team from the States at the BMMA hospital in Sula. One night the emergency room nurse woke us for two stab wound patients. One patient was eviscerated and needed blood badly. Being O negative and the only persona able or willing, I gave. Two units, as he needed a lot of blood. The man survived two and one half hours of surgery losing nearly half his blood volume. Two days later I visited with the man and was able to lead him to Christ. The same afternoon Joshua gave blood to another patient.

November 9, 1996 – Gave blood to hospital in Santa Rosa so that neighbor boy could have operation. Boy's father and mother were too scared but hospital would not operate without having a unit of blood. I feel a little weak this evening.

December 1, 1996 – Used our truck as hearse for funeral of neighbor lady. I was able to witness to the family over the next few days. Two professions of faith resulted from the assisting with this funeral.

January 3, 1997 – A 68 year-old man stepped in front of me on highway near San Pedro Sula. He suffered a broken leg and concussion. Police and witnesses stated that the fault was with the pedestrian. However, Honduran law states that driver of vehicle always pays for damages. After lengthy discussions with police, family, and lawyer, I paid L1300 ($100) for damages and L77 ($7) for medical expenses. The price was originally less, but because I'm a North American I had to pay more. Not a good experience, but I learned a lot.

March 18, 1997 – Hosted construction and medical team from Charlotte, Virginia. Saw patients and dug and constructed outhouses and latrines.

everyday life

IT HELPS TO BE CRAZY!

March 24, 1997 – Started teaching Emergency Medical Technician course to Red Cross volunteers. Interviewed by local radio program. Given chance to talk about Christ while on the air. A couple came to home asking about Jesus after hearing program.

April 22, 1997 – Lawyer who was helping us to obtain our residences is in jail for theft. Have to find new one and start whole process over again.

May 15, 1998 – Received our papers indicating that we are now permanent residents of Honduras. Thank you, Lord.

chapter eight

JOSÉ

One of the projects that we had in mind after our initial trips to Honduras was to set up a nutrition program for malnourished children. Honduras is the second poorest country in the Western Hemisphere and starvation is an everyday occurrence. We felt the desire to do as Christ did when he walked the earth and that was to try and relieve a little of the suffering.

The nutrition program feeds, provides medical care, vitamins, and personal hygiene products for many, many children every day. It also allows opportunities for education. Though the program is a wonderful and certainly appreciated ministry it is designed to be a door opener for the entrance of Christ into the lives of many whom might not hear the gospel through other means. The family of José is an example.

In late 1997 we heard of a family who had moved into a house a couple of kilometers back in the woods behind our home. We heard of this news after a couple of tragic deaths. Two young daughters of the family had starved to death. I immediately made my way to the family homestead and found the mother and father working in the cornfield. I told them about the program and told them that their children under age twelve were welcome to come to our home and be part of the nutrition program. They were very pleased and said they would send down three of their children.

The next day Jose and two of his sisters were there for lunch. José was a little guy about six years old. Though it was very obvious that he had never owned a pair of shoes nor more than one change of clothes at any time in his life, he was all smiles, just as cute as can be. He smiled from ear to ear. You couldn't help but to fall in love with the kid.

After about six months on the program, José and his sisters were looking better and were much healthier. One day, one of our neighbors knocked on the door and told me that Jose's father wanted me to meet him at his house. So I made the walk back to their home. I was met by Jose's father and invited into the house. It really wasn't much of a house: a fifteen by ten foot adobe structure. No electricity, no water, a cooking pit outside served as the kitchen. This served as home for a family of seven. There was a small torch, which provided light inside the structure. As I entered I noticed that Jose's mother was lying in a make shift bed. Jose's father shook my hand and made small talk. He then told me that his wife was sick with cancer and was dying. He said that she knew this and that she told him that she wanted to talk with someone about God before her death. He went on to tell me that he offered to go up into the town and bring down the Catholic priest. He said that she told him no. She told him that she wanted to talk with the missionary up the path who not only talked about God and Jesus but also helped the people. Tears filled my eyes. I made my way to her bedside and started speaking with her. Some twenty minutes and a prayer later the angels were praising as another lost soul was saved.

Over the next three weeks or so either myself or someone from our mission would go and read the Bible to her daily. When she passed on I was asked to conduct the funeral. It was the first evangelical funeral the local people had ever attended. I preached Jesus that afternoon. And because of that funeral, several of that sweet lady's nieces, nephews and cousins started attending our mission and several accepted Christ in the following weeks.

That's why Christ helped to feed the lost who were hungry. Doing so opens the doors to those whose stomachs are filled by the food He provides. Because someone cared enough for a little guy named José to help to provide him with some meals, his mother and many of his relatives found Christ.

chapter nine

CLINIC WORK

The other door-opening ministry that we became involved with was a medical ministry. Being involved with medical care since I was sixteen years old, I certainly had a great interest in it and knew that people, especially here in Honduras, would be receptive to such help. And once you start talking to folks about their physical problems it is real easy to open the door to their spiritual life – thus the medical ministry.

The Honduran Ministry of Health looked over my credentials and licensed me as a physician assistant. We had a makeshift clinic behind the house in what were the maid's quarters. The medicine was donated and/or purchased through the gifts of individuals, medical teams, groups, and Baptist Medical Ministries International (a separate ministry of the BMAA). We saw non-emergency patients a couple of days a week at the clinic and emergencies whenever I was home. We also made trips out into the smaller villages of western Honduras on a regular basis. We would see two to three hundred patients a week; a lot of common ailments along with a good amount of diseases that are found only in the tropics. We also treated serious emergencies including lacerations, broken bones, and burns. It was pretty much your everyday, family practice. Our clinic was open for those who could not pay to see a local physician. Again, this medical ministry was a door opener for the Gospel as the next couple of stories illustrate.

Gloribell, a sixteen year-old young lady, came to the clinic one morning because of headaches. It was obvious by her actions, her words, and her body language that much more was going on than just a few headaches. As I questioned her the truth slowly came out. She was depressed, depressed because she felt unworthy. Her parents and grandmother had joined a very charismatic group of Christians and she had been going with them for some time to these meetings. The problem was that while most of the adults, including her family, had at one time or another spoke in 'tongues', she had never received this 'gift'. This coupled with the fact that she suffered from temptations, which the charismatic leaders told her she would not be having if she were a good Christian, caused her to feel unworthy and unchristian.

These feelings led to her depression. After counseling with her for some time I invited her to come to our mission and become involved with our young people. Our mission has a large group of young people and depression was something these kids did not suffer from. She fit in very quickly as the kids made her feel welcome. She became one of our helpers in our AWANAs youth program. She found the assurance of her salvation and came to understand that not every person has or receives the same gifts and talents from God.

Luis, Patty, and their three-year-old daughter showed up at the clinic one morning with a few common physical ailments. As I treated them I began to talk with them. I found out that they had been married for five years and at the moment were having some martial problems. This opened the door. I counseled them for a while and invited them to church. I also gave them a tract. They said goodbye and promised to come to church. That afternoon, Luis came back and wanted to know if I could visit them that evening in their home. Sure, I could. When I arrived, Luis had his New Testament out and the tract. He had been reading the tract and suggested verses and said that he wanted to get saved right then. He felt the Holy Spirit leading him. So he prayed and got saved right there, right then. He was baptized into the mission three weeks later. Patty was saved and baptized a short time later. They became very faithful and active in the Lord's work.

That was how the medical ministry worked. By easing physical pain, the patient became more aware of their heart pain and their need for a healing of the heart and soul.

chapter ten

THE BIG GRINGO

During our first couple of years in Santa Rosa I had the opportunity to befriend two Honduran army officers. They helped me with paperwork problems and I was acting as the army base medic. One day they came by the house and asked if I would be willing to go with them on a humanitarian aid mission. They would provide a lot of medicine if I would go along and help to see patients. This was going to be a large project with two Honduran physicians, a dentist, and me, if I was able to go. This sounded like a great opportunity to see some new places and meet some new people. I said sure.

Two days later I was picked up in an army truck and we headed off into the mountains. We traveled about an hour on the paved highway before we turned off onto a rock road. We traveled this good road for another hour and a half. Then things started getting interesting. We were heading up Mount Celaque, the highest peak in Honduras at 10,000 feet. The road kept getting steeper, narrower, and rougher. Soon the road had become a trail so narrow that the vehicle passed with an inch clearance between the sheer, rock wall on one side, and the straight-down cliff on the other. I was certainly catching up on my prayer time during this trip.

After about three and a half hours from the time we left the house, we arrived at a fairly large, but very remote, indigenous village. These people were of the Lenca tribes who have been occupying these mountains for the past 2,500 years. It was here that we setup for two days of work. I noticed right away that the people, especially the children, seemed to be drawn to me. Being three-fourths kid myself, I had no trouble developing a rapport with these young people. They told me that I was the first white man who had ever visited their village. And since these people rarely left their village I was the first white man that most of them had ever seen.

The people were wonderful to help us in setting up the clinic areas. We used the village community building as our headquarters. They brought candles and kerosene lamps for us to have light; they hauled water and boiled it for us to drink and to have for bathing. They prepared beans, rice, tortilla, and chicken for us to eat. They really went all out. And we worked. We

iT HELPS TO BE CRAZY!

worked hard seeing and treating patients. We worked until a storm drove everybody inside. And what a storm it was. Most of the storm was below us. We were looking down and into the clouds as the streaks of lightening passed within what seemed like inches of us. It was such a strange and beautiful sight. The rain then started and the raindrops drumming on the clay tile roofs provided a wonderful rhythm to sleep to.

The next morning started early as we saw more patients. People were coming from more distant villages for treatment. In the two days that we were there, the two physicians, the dentist, and myself saw and treated 800 patients.

That afternoon we begin to pack up and prepare for our trip back to Santa Rosa. The village people jumped right in and were doing their best to assist us. However, the boxes of equipment and supplies were heavy and these people are not very big. The average man is about 5'3" and the ladies are around 4'6". Due to heredity and poor nutrition, these people just do not grow very big. I was a giant among them standing at 6 feet and weighing in at 250 pounds. But they tried their best to help out. As I was playing with some of the kids I noticed a group of four men trying to pick up this box of supplies. The box was large and they were having a tough time with it. Not wanting the box to fall, I ran over and kind of grabbed the box out of their hands and put it in the truck by myself. The men and kids just kind of stepped back and said, "O-o-o-o-h!" Now that was kind of fun. So I went over picked up another box and put it on the truck. "A-a-a-h!" went the crowd. Now the kids started shouting and waving to other kids and their parents to come watch the big, strong gringo move the heavy boxes all by himself. Soon the village square was full of people watching me pick up boxes. I had an audience. And what do missionaries do when they have an audience? They preach. So that is just what I started to do. Now I can't say for certain that anyone was saved after that short sermon, but they heard about Jesus and I received an invitation to go back to that village to tell them more about the Christ who is a lot stronger than this big gringo.

chapter eleven

FURLOUGH

In late June 1998, we returned to the States for a furlough. A great time of visiting family, making new friends and renewing old ones.

Furlough Is…
...using up the 12,000-mile warranty on your new-to-you, used van in four months;
...being taken to a restaurant with a 200-foot buffet and your young daughter crying because there are no black beans and rice to eat;
...becoming a platinum member of Holiday Inn's Priority Club in three months;
...saying that it's great to be here in the First Baptist Church of Magnolia when you're at the Second Baptist Church of Springhill;
...dropping your oldest child off at college and then crying the whole 300-mile trip to the next appointment as you realize what you have just done;
...calling back to Honduras and being told that everything is going just great as if you had never left;
...realizing that home is truly were the heart is and home is 2000 miles away in a different country.

chapter twelve

ARMY DUTY

We arrived back home in Honduras on January 5, 1999. Our friends met us with open arms and we settled back down very quickly.

Before I left on furlough I had been asked to serve as a chaplain at the local army base. The last Sunday afternoon of January, one of the officers whom I had become friends with stopped by the house. He asked if I was free the following Tuesday in order to come by the base and meet the new commanding officer. I said it would be an honor and so made plans.

Tuesday, when I arrived at the fort, (it is the original fort built in Spanish style about a hundred a fifty years ago) I was ushered into the Colonel's office and had a nice visit with him. He told me that he felt it was important that his men receive spiritual instruction to go along with their regular military training. He then asked me if I would be able to come weekly and give Bible lessons and talk with the men. Of course I jumped at this opportunity! As we concluded the meeting and I was preparing to leave, he then asked me if I would stay for a change of command ceremony in which he would be formally accepting his new command and responsibilities. This type of ceremony is a very formal and special event in any army officer's career.

As the five hundred plus soldiers and officers gathered on the parade field, to my surprise I was escorted to the podium with the higher-ranking officers. After the battalion was called to attention I was introduced to give an invocation. Though someone had failed to advise me of this task, I was able to perform this mission. I then sat down and enjoyed the ceremony as it progressed. As the Colonel was concluding his speech to his men that included his goals, plans, and ideas for the battalion, he then told them that a soldier cannot be the best soldier possible without God's blessings and doing God's will. Then, to my surprise, he asked me to come and preach to him and to his men from God's word. Fortunately, I did have a New Testament in my pocket, and as I stumbled to the microphone, I thought of the first sermon I ever preached, the story of Nicodemis. I explained to these soldiers that everyone needs salvation and that the lowest private is equal to his new

army duty
IT HELPS TO BE CRAZY!

colonel in the eyes of God. This brought a lot of smiles from the ranks and a few from the officers. The Colonel even grinned a bit.

After the ceremony several officers came to me asking when they could talk with me in private about the Bible and salvation. The Colonel even asked when we could visit again. I told him to just give me a date. He did so and weekly Bible studies were planned.

For that first meeting nearly all the officers and the Colonel were present along with about 150 soldiers. One of the officers came to me and made plans to visit with me the next week. He said that he was like an ox looking for a drink of water.

I met with that officer the next week in his office. He told me that on the night of that first meeting, late, after all the rest of the base had gone to sleep, he asked Christ to save him. And he was only the first. These weekly Bible studies soon became worship services on Sunday mornings. And not just at the one base but a second one also. It was not long before two other officers accepted Christ along with several soldiers. These men started nightly devotionals in the barracks, which led to other professions of faith. It is just unbelievable to see how God can take a simple friendship and use it so mightily.

Over the next several years I had opportunity to develop many relationships within the Honduran military. Preaching and teaching at the area army bases were a regular part of my week. There even times that I accompanied army units on combat missions, serving as chaplain always, and occasionally as a medic.

One day, while I was taking a siesta, one of the kids woke me and told me that some army officers were outside looking for me. As I stepped out of the house I was met by the military commander of the entire western half of Honduras and a large assembly of other officers, our town's mayor, television news crews and reporters.

The senior colonel, whom I had met before, quickly smiled broadly, relieving a bit of my unease, but I was still taken aback.

As the lights came on, the colonel began making a short speech about how appreciative the military community, the president of Honduras, and the people of Honduras were for the physical and spiritual assistance that we had given over the past several years. He then motioned for one of his staff from which he took a couple of envelopes. From one of the envelopes, he took a letter and a certificate stating that the government and military department of Honduras was presenting me with a commission as a military officer. He went on to explain that this was a very rarely given to civilians and had never

IT HELPS TO BE CRAZY!

been presented to a non-Honduran before. This was one of the few times that I had ever been shocked into silence. The colonel then opened the other envelope and read from the gold embossed ivory paper. It was an invitation from the President of Honduras to attend a state dinner. My family and I were to be guests of honor at the Presidential Palace

And here I stood barefoot, mouth agape, and television cameras recording my reaction. Sometimes God will humble us with His not-so-pleasant ways. Other times, the humbling is more amusing and enjoyable.

Sunday School on the Porch

Valerie teaching the Armor of God

Main Street in Santa Rosa Copán

*Tom, the Big Gringo, with Herman
Attending Patients in a Mountain Village*

Youth Service at Santa Rosa Mission

The Garifuna Village of Miami

A Beach Baptism

A Mission Building in the Mountains...

...and a Worship Service in that Building

Tom with National Missionaries and Pastors in El Salvador (Noé is on the left)

Service in Vera Cruz after the Earthquake

Noé Teaching Children's Bible Class

A Mission in San Salvador

IT HELPS TO BE CRAZY!

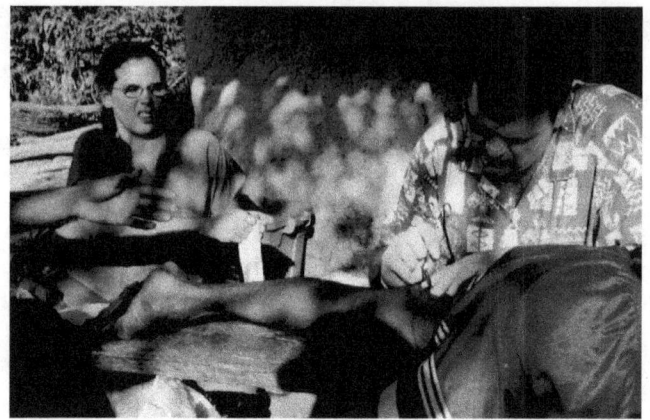

Tom and Dalaina Removing "The Bullet"

*The Jopling Family,
Colonel Herman Alfaro and his Family,
and Honduran President Ricardo Maduro
at the Presidential Palace*

At a Nutrition Program Location

IT HELPS TO BE CRAZY!

The New Watchman and Family

You have to love them...

chapter thirteen

A FUNERAL, A NEW BIRTH, AND A COUPLE OF WEDDINGS

The Friday before Easter I performed a funeral for one of our Miraflores mission members. One of our teenagers drowned while swimming with his brother and friends. This young man had been saved and baptized about a year before. As the Bible tells us, all things turn out good for those who love Christ and God can use anything for His glory. This death and funeral was no exception.

I arrived at the family's home, the teenager's father, who was not a Christian and was a bad alcoholic, ran to me. He never let me out of arm's reach until several hours after the funeral. He was a broken man, sobered by the death of his son.

At the graveside, I gave a short sermon. I also prayed that if there be anyone present that was not saved that they would be miserable, unable to eat, sleep, or to have peace until that someone accepted Christ. Four days after the funeral, the father came to see me. God had answered that prayer. This man who had lost jobs, been in jail, seen his family suffer and go hungry because of his drinking, came asking for salvation and the help of God to give up alcohol. He told me that he had not slept more than a dozen hours and had not been able to eat since the death of his son. He told me that he had been broken and wanted God to repair him. In our front yard, he found the best mechanic, Jesus.

He remained sober. He attended church services, read the Bible, and his family members told me that he became a completely new person. There is an old saying that every time the bells ring for a funeral, they also ring for a birth. It certainly held true this time.

Love is the same all over the world and I had the honor of performing a couple of weddings in two of our more remote missions.

The first was in the village of Corlatina. This young couple had been living together for the past three years and had two children. They both had accepted Christ in the past few months and greatly wanted to become

*a funeral, a new birth,
and a couple of weddings*

IT HELPS TO BE CRAZY!

disciples. They realized that the first thing they needed to do was to become husband and wife and so the stage was set.

I was invited to officiate and the pastor of our Miraflores mission was invited to preach a short message before the vows. Please realize that these were the first Christian weddings that these villages had ever experienced. It was a candle light ceremony (no electricity), the bride dressed in her finest dress (she only had two dresses), and the groom wore his new cowboy hat as he rode up on his burro.

The air was thick as over 50 invited and uninvited guests, 4 dogs, a couple of chickens, and a piglet filled the small room. As Manual was concluding his short 45-minute sermon, he told the story of a man and a woman whom he knew that had been married for 35 years before the woman's death. He told us of how miserable the husband had been for the entire 35 years because the woman was so overbearing. He ended this story by telling us that he finally saw the husband smile as the police led him away after he had strangled his overbearing wife. I'm still not exactly sure what Manuel wanted us to learn from that story.

I then took over the ceremony and led the couple through their vows. The rings were exchanged after we found them among the pine straw and sawdust where the three-year-old daughter had dropped them. As the groom kissed his beaming wife, her father shouted a loud whoop, ran outside and set-off the stick of dynamite that he had been hiding under his shirt.

The next week I was in Potrerillos, again to assist with the vows. The building was filled with beautiful flowers and people. The ceremony began with us all singing about 27 songs and hymns as the groom was 45 minutes late.

Finally, the groom entered with his best man and then the bride entered. She was dressed in a beautiful, long, white gown, her face was perfectly made up, and her hair was freshly cut and styled. I had never seen her so beautiful. Apparently, neither had the groom as he fainted at the sight of her and we had to quickly find a chair for him to sit in. In order not to make the groom feel too awkward, we also found a chair for the bride to sit in beside her perspiring groom. The chairs turned out to be very handy as the local pastor also preached a short 45-minute message.

At some point during the message, I heard that the groom had forgotten the marriage license and the ring. Having the only vehicle within 10 miles, I quickly grabbed the groom's father and sped down the goat trail that led to

*a funeral, a new birth,
and a couple of weddings*

IT HELPS TO BE CRAZY!

their home where we recovered the forgotten items and then sped back to the temple just as the pastor was asking for my whereabouts.

After the ceremony, I was invited to the reception where I ate some of the best-roasted goat you could ever ask for.

Who says weddings are boring?

IT HELPS TO BE CRAZY!

chapter fourteen

THEY CAME BY TWO AND THREES

I was visiting one of our mission nutrition program sites one day...

...Shortly before midday they started arriving. Most came in groups of two or three, running, laughing, and talking rapidly. A few came up on their burros or mules, jumping down from atop bags of corn and coffee beans that were tied to the backs of their pack animals. Though their clothes were old, tattered, and mostly soiled, and only a few of them had real shoes, they were excited and smiling. Some came with a sibling, a couple of orphans walked up alone. Each of the children also carried a stick of firewood in one hand and a brightly colored toothbrush in the other. As they reached the front door of the adobe house they formed a line and continued their animated conversations.

Inside the house, three ladies of the local mission were putting the finishing touches on that day's meal. One lady was using two stones to grind the boiled corn into a mushy paste. Another was patting the paste into palm-sized tortillas and placing them onto the hot metal stove top to cook. The third lady was stirring the refried beans and the rice, potato, and vegetable mixture. Though it was damp and cool outside – the altitude is almost 6,000 feet – the kitchen was very toasty from the wood cooking fire.

Soon the mission pastor arrived. He went into the house to see if everything was coming along. Being assured that everything was okay and on schedule, he then began to allow the children to file into the dining room. As they passed by the pastor he made sure that they placed their stick of firewood on to a growing pile – this was their meal ticket. The children removed the chairs from the top of the table and found their seats. When all were still and quiet the pastor opened a large book of illustrated Bible stories. He read of Abraham's test of faith as Abraham tied his son to the altar. The children's eyes widened, a few mouths dropped open, and you could hear many deep breaths being taken as one when the pastor read of the knife in Abraham's hand being raised above his young son. When they heard that God had stopped Abraham at the last moment their breaths were exhaled as one.

IT HELPS TO BE CRAZY!

Smiles once again appeared on their faces. Quickly, the pastor finished the story and young voices once again filled the air.

The ladies had now started to fill plates with the prepared food. Milk was placed in cups. The plates and cups were placed before the children. When everyone had their meal before them, the pastor asked the children to stand and then he led them in prayer. As soon as they said the last Amen, they sat back down and then only the sounds of their eating could be heard. While the children were eating, one of the ladies passed by and handed out vitamins to each child. It wasn't long until the first of the children had finished their meals. After eating the children pulled out those brightly colored toothbrushes and went to the pastor. The pastor had retrieved a tube of toothpaste from a shelf and then placed a dollop onto their toothbrushes as they came to him. The toothbrushes were then taken out back near the *pila* (general purpose water tank and wash area) where the children brushed their teeth and washed their hands.

By now all of the children had finished their meals. A couple of the children volunteered to gather the dishes and to clean the eating area. As this was going on, a couple of the ladies washed up the pots and dishes while the other straightened up the rest of the kitchen. The corn grinding stones were cleaned, the firewood stacked, everything was dried, wiped, and made ready for tomorrow. The next morning, a different group of ladies would take their turn at preparing and serving the meal. As the ladies left, the last of the children could be seen going down the various trails to their own homes in the village. A few would stop and wave to their friends and to the ladies. One little girl had stopped on the trail. As we caught up to her she ran to us, stopped directly in our path, and looked up at us with big brown eyes and a smile. "Gracias", was all she said before running into her home.

Nothing else needed to be said.

IT HELPS TO BE CRAZY!

chapter fifteen

A DAY WITH NOÉ

It is Wednesday, about 7 o'clock in the evening. His two children are finishing up their homework and getting ready for bed; his wife has not made it home from work. The streets of San Salvador are still full of traffic and the sounds of the city make their way into their upstairs apartment, but not so much as to disturb his study and thoughts. Noé sits down at the dining table. He has gathered tomorrow's lesson for the adults that he will be teaching along with his Bible dictionary, concordance, and some other reference books that he collected back during his seminary days. Noé likes to be well prepared and he knows that his class is very interested in what he teaches. About nine o'clock his wife makes her way in from work. They both are tired and so they retire for the evening.

It is now 9:00 Thursday morning. The kids have left for school and his wife has left for work. Noé now has a little time to prepare today's lessons for the children's Bible study. He takes time to read over the lesson and teacher's guide. He colors, cuts out, and glues together the visuals and teaching aids that goes with the lesson. Once that is done, he gets the lesson handout and activity page and walks six blocks to a small bookstore where he gets copies made. By the time he gets back he has just enough time for a quick lunch before it will be time to leave.

At noon, Noé walks out the door with a backpack full of lessons, crayons, scissors, his Bible, and other materials that he will need for today's lessons. It is only a short walk to the bus stop where he begins his trip. A 20 minute ride on the first bus takes him to a large terminal where he catches another bus. This second bus ride is longer and it is more uncomfortable. The bus is filled beyond capacity and not just with people. Live chickens and ducks, fresh vegetables, plywood, several bags of cement, and some not so fresh fish are among some of the things that have found their way onto the bus. At least all of the windows are open so the hour long ride is bearable.

Noé exits the bus at an intersection of a couple of small roads. Now it is time to walk or hitch a ride. After walking about a mile, a pickup comes by and offers Noé a ride. Throwing the backpack in the bed of the truck Noé climbs in. The truck goes within a mile of the village where the mission point is. Noé climbs out and offers the driver a couple of coins which are quickly accepted. He starts off down the dirt trail, dodging the mud holes and the animal droppings as much as possible, though not always successfully.

a day with noé

IT HELPS TO BE CRAZY!

It is now close to 2:30 as Noé makes his way to the house. About twenty children between the ages of four and fifteen years old have already gathered and are waiting for him. They start to yell in excitement and several run to meet him, shaking his hand and offering to help him with his backpack. Other children in the nearby houses hear the yells and they began coming in small clusters of two or three. They bring buckets, chairs, boards, and other things in which to sit on. Noé and the children make their way to an area beneath some trees. Once the commotion has died down some, Noé takes a seat and calls roll. He calls out about forty names and someone yells "present" to nearly each one. After the roll is checked Noé starts singing. What his voice may lack in tone quality, it is made up for in volume and happiness. The kids join in. Several fun and happy songs are sung. Most of the songs have a Bible story or principle within them. The singing and joking goes on for 20 minutes or so, during which kids are still arriving. The children's enthusiasm is not dampened by their obvious state of poverty; not a single shoe or untorn shirt or blouse is found in the crowd. Now it is time for prayer and this week's lesson. Noé leads them all in a prayer that is repeated by the children. After making sure everyone is quiet and seated he begins the lesson. He tells the story of an Old Testament Jewish king that was sick and then was healed by God after repenting of his sins. He uses the visuals that he prepared earlier to make the story easier for the kids to understand. The kids are asked to repeat parts of the story and are quizzed to make sure they understand and that they are listening. After the lesson, Noé gets the activity pages and the crayons and scissors out of the backpack. The lessons are passed out and each child receives one crayon. None of the crayons are whole; rather they are halves and less than halves. The children pass the crayon pieces around among themselves until all are satisfied with their masterpieces. As they finish the coloring process they take turns with the scissors cutting out the figures. When all have completed their activity page, Noé leads them in a final prayer. After the prayer, Noé reaches once again into his backpack and pulls out a bag of suckers that he had purchased the day before. Noé walks around and hands a sucker to each child. The children, as they leave with their suckers in mouth and their colored masterpieces and "chairs" in hand, wave bye and yell, "Thank you! See you next week!"

After the children leave, Noé readies himself and the area for the arrival of the adults. He has about an hour before time to start their lesson.

It is now five o'clock. About fifteen adults and older teenagers have gathered in the area beneath the trees. Though it is thundering, it looks as if the rain will hold off for an hour or so. Noé has pulled out some small hymnals from the seemingly bottomless backpack. As they are passed out Noé calls out a page number and then begins to sing in the same loud voice as before. The lack of musical instruments does not lessen the joy in the songs. Prayer requests and blessings are shared among the group and prayer is offered. Noé then begins to teach from a passage in Romans. He relates Paul's teachings to the people gathered in this group. Questions are raised and Noé not only answers the questions but helps the group to discover the answers for themselves. At the end of the lesson, Noé speaks of the Gospel and Jesus and salvation. Heads are bowed and eyes are closed. As the final prayer is led by Noé, he gives an invitation to those that might be lost or to those that might have a heavy heart to stay and visit with him after the lesson. After the prayer a final song is sung and then the people begin to leave. Everyone shakes everyone else's hand.

All have left – all except for one lady. She is still sitting in her chair. She is looking down at her feet. Noé sits down next to her. He asks what he can do for her. She says that she knows that she is lost and would like to be saved. Noé opens his Bible and they read several verses together. Noé questions and she answers. She understands what is needed to be saved. She wants to pray for that salvation. Noé prays and then she does. When the prayers are over, both have tears rolling down their cheeks but they both are smiling from ear to ear. Noé visits with her for a few more minutes. She promises to be back next week. When she leaves she is no longer looking down at her feet but she is looking up and smiling.

Noé gathers the hymnals and his Bible and packs them into his backpack. The thunder is louder now and the raindrops start to fall. It is nearly dark. Noé pulls out an umbrella, opens it, and starts out on the trail back home. By the time Noé has made it out to the road, it is completely dark. There are no headlights in either direction. The rain is harder now. Noé adjusts his backpack on his shoulders and starts off. It's only five miles to the bus stop. And perhaps next week it won't be raining.

Noé is a missionary pastor in El Salvador with whom I had opportunity to labor with. Though this is the actual story of one day I shared in Noe's life, this story is not unique. There are native missionary pastors and church planters throughout Central and South America whose daily experiences are much like those of Noé. I don't think that requesting a prayer for them is too much to ask for.

chapter sixteen

CHURCH PLANTING: CARIBBEAN STYLE

As the plane pulls to a stop you see several men pushing an old set of steps up to the door of the plane. You step off and enter a terminal that reminds you of something you saw in old black and white movie. You walk outside and notice that the policeman also looks like someone out of a Hollywood film, dressed in a crisp, white tropical uniform. The postcard scenery of the surrounding jungle, the beaches, and crystal clear waters of the Caribbean Sea further lend themselves to the idea that you have just stepped back in time and out of the rat race that most of us are involved in.

This is the country of Belize. It is a small country that borders Mexico, Guatemala, and the Caribbean with former ties to Great Britain. Belize is like eating a plate of beans and rice with hot sauce on top for a little kick and a cup of Earl Grey tea on the side for a touch of mellowness.

As you walk through downtown Belize City the words and languages of the people are one of the first things you notice. You hear English spoken with a Caribbean accent. You hear Creole and Spanish. You then hear a language that sounds like something that reminds you of Africa. This is the language of the Garifunas. You then hear languages that are Arabic and Oriental sounding. All of these different languages are being spoken by people within an area of just a couple of blocks.

Belize's population of 210,000 is as almost as varied as the country's bird population. Descendants of slaves, the indigenous Mayas, European Spanish colonists, and English colonists are the largest ethnic groups. However, there is a large and growing population of Lebanese and Taiwanese immigrants. With the varied native population, immigrants and the tourists that come from all over the world to enjoy the physical attributes of Belize you have a the makings of real melting pot and thus making Belize City one of the most cosmopolitan cities in Central America.

The Garifuna people, descendants of slaves that originally made their way throughout Central America from Honduras, live very close to the sea; both physically and culturally. They also enjoy traveling. These cultural traits and Belize's natural geography combined to make Belize a destination of many

church planting: caribbean style
IT HELPS TO BE CRAZY!

Garifunas. Over the past several years hundreds of single men and whole families have left their native homes in Honduras and have moved to Belize. More recently many of those who have made the move were believers and members of evangelical churches. Though most of them have continued to practice their faith as individuals, there has not been any real movement to organize missions or churches among the Garifuna community in Belize. That was until Brother Ricardo came to Belize.

Brother Ricardo Herrera is the mission coordinator among the Garifuna people. He has worked for several years in planting churches and assisting other church planters. A few of Brother Ricardo's fellow church members were among those who moved to Belize. Being the good pastor that he is, Brother Ricardo decided to maintain contact with those distant members. To keep up this contact he had to make some trips to Belize, long trips that took several days over land and by boat. These contacts soon lead to other contacts. Before long, a number of acquaintances, friendships, and relationships had developed – enough to firm the idea that a church planting effort might be feasible in Belize City.

The Garifuna community in Belize City is among the poorest of the city's 70,000 inhabitants. Their neighborhood is mostly set upon land-fill that two years ago was brine backwater next to the local harbor and port. Mud, mosquitoes, and the smell of rank, salt-water marshes meet you before you ever really get to the people's homes. The homes are built upon pilings and poles that stick up out of the mud. Walkways are rotten planks set upon low dikes, levees, and nailed to the top of shorter poles and pilings. This is part of Belize that you never see on the postcards. This is where God lead Brother Ricardo to plant a New Testament church among his people.

A year or so before, Brother Ricardo began to make visits every three months. The stay would be for ten to fourteen days during which he would lead Bible studies in the individual homes of families. There were four families, about ten people, in the beginning and the meetings were usually in the evening after those who worked had returned home. He would rotate through each family so that three studies were conducted in each home during his stay. Soon neighbors began to come to the studies and the small homes were filled with people listening and participating in the studies. Believers began to enjoy Christian fellowship again and professions of faith from new converts began to happen.

Now those four small groups have grown to seven larger groups with about fifty people making up these groups. Each group has a leader that oversees and teaches the group members. Brother Ricardo's role has now changed to that of teacher and mentor to the group leaders. Now when he visits he concentrates on expanding the knowledge and leadership abilities of the group leaders and then watches them as they share what they have learned with their groups. Following the example of Christ, instead of trying to Shepard the whole flock by himself, he instead disciples a smaller group and then each of them disciples others.

Over the past year the groups have been busy in other ways. They made application and have received recognition from the government to form a church. One of the group leaders is in the process of translating the church planting program into Garifuna. Three group leaders have begun an extension Bible Institute program. Two group leaders have a ninety-minute radio program every Sunday which is heard throughout most of Belize. The program targets the Garifuna people. Several new converts have been baptized and several more are completing initial discipleship classes so that can be baptized. The group leaders and Brother Ricardo have formed a committee and to investigate believers who would like to join the mission by statement or letter. While things often move slowly in Central America, these folks have not been letting time idle away.

The fledging mission recently held their first open meeting for all the groups together. The last rays of the sun were reflecting off the nearby waves. Reggae and calypso music could be heard from most every house. The assembled group leaders were setting up chairs on a small area of firm ground near one of their homes. An extension cord was stretched to which was wired a light bulb. Another group leader arrived carrying a keyboard under his arm. Some batteries were found and put into the keyboard. As the musician warmed up people began to show up in small groups. Greetings and introductions were made. "Hellos" and "How are you" greetings were said in four different languages - English, Garifuna, Spanish, and Creole. Soon there were forty or so people present. After a few minutes, the group leader who had been assigned to direct this first meeting asked everyone to find a place but to remain standing. Brother Ricardo was asked to come to the front and to open this first service with a prayer. As Brother Ricardo prayed the others did also. The assembled voices in different languages began to give thanks to God for the many blessings that He had given them. And they asked for grace and the opportunity to be a new light for those walking in darkness.

IT HELPS TO BE CRAZY!

chapter seventeen

EARTHQUAKE!

On afternoon of Saturday, January 13, 2001, the country of El Salvador was jolted with an earthquake that we felt at our home in Honduras (7.7 Richter scale). We immediately attempted to establish communication with our churches, missions, and people in El Salvador. Communication was impossible. The following note was written the night of the January 17th upon returning from El Salvador:

I just arrived back from El Salvador and thought that I would update what is going on over there.

I left early Sunday morning with fellow pastor Manuel Pinto and two other younger men. The drive into San Salvador was without incident. In the capital, we begin to notice damage. Just outside the capital we were diverted from the main highway to a very rough secondary road that runs across a lava field at the base of a volcano. The main highway was closed due to landslides. We finally arrived in the early afternoon in the village of Vera Cruz, about 25 miles northwest of San Salvador. This village also sits at the base of a different volcano. (Several of the volcanoes in the area have become much more active since the earthquake.) The village is a very poor one with nearly all the houses being adobe and the people living off the land. Brother Rafael Garcia is the pastor of the church there. After being assured that he and his family were okay we immediately headed into the main area of the village. We were then greeted by the village elders who gave is a tour of the area. There was no loss of life in this village and only a few minor injuries, however, the buildings suffered greatly. Of the 50 homes in the village, 46 had been destroyed or heavily damaged. The church building was also heavily damaged. I was told that no one from the government, Red Cross, military, or any other organization had yet been there. The people of the village were still in complete shock and were terrorized by every aftershock. (As of this morning, some 1000 aftershocks had been recorded with the largest being 5.4 on the Richter scale.) They were basically paralyzed and looking for some guidance. With what daylight we had left, we organized a couple of teams to *earthquake!*

IT HELPS TO BE CRAZY!

survey and list the needs of each family in order that we might have a better idea of what was before us.

We finally lay down under the stars for a little rest around midnight. Most of our sleep was robbed by the aftershocks. We were up at first light Monday morning. After a hot sponge bath in a nearby river (the volcanic activity had heated the water) we began organizing work crews; teams to begin salvage and clean-up work, a team to cook, a team to secure necessary supplies.

We then headed for the city of Santa Ana. There we purchased beans, rice, and other food items along with heavy duty plastic, tarps, and medicine. Communications were still down at this time. After securing the supplies, we headed back to Vera Cruz and formed another group to begin distributing the supplies and constructing lean-to shelters from the plastic and tarps.

About midday we headed to the other end of El Salvador. Again we had to take several detours due to landslides and damaged areas. We arrived in Ozatlan around 5:30 p.m. and met Pastor David. Ozatlan is a large town of several thousand occupants. Here, there were fatalities and more injuries. This town was also heavily damaged with about 80% of the structures being severely damaged or destroyed. The church building was totally destroyed along with most of the member's homes. The El Salvadoran army was present here to prevent looting and to bring in water, but no other assistance was evident. After a survey of the village, we again met with town elders to begin formulating some plans. We had purchased beans, rice, tarps, and plastic earlier as we passed through San Salvador. Teams were organized to begin distributing these items to the neediest. Numerous strong aftershocks and the falling of roof tiles and adobe walls punctuated another fitful night under the stars.

Early Tuesday morning we organized salvage and clean up teams and got them going. We then headed back to San Salvador to purchase more supplies and to check on the church at Santa Tecla. Santa Tecla was the area of greatest loss of life. Most of the deaths occurred when a landslide of gigantic proportions completely covered and crushed several blocks of a very densely populated neighborhood. However, the BMA church in Santa Tecla did not suffer any casualties and only had minor ceiling damage and one wall had been weakened. After a long day of driving, looking for supplies that were becoming hard to find, fighting with poor communications, and being stalled by landslides, we finally arrived back in Vera Cruz at 9:00 p.m. After a couple more organizational meetings and unloading supplies, we finally laid down after midnight. If there were stars out that night, we did not know it because not even the aftershocks disturbed our sleep.

We left Vera Cruz, headed back to Ozatlan at 5:30 am Wednesday in order to beat the traffic tie-ups. When we arrived in Ozatlan, we were surprised to see the difference that 24 hours had made. Brother David told us that as the teams of youth from the church went about salvage and clean up, the other folks in town asked what they were doing. The youth told them that they were not going to just sit around any longer waiting on the government, but that they were going to start trying to get things back to normal. The idea apparently caught on and by the afternoon nearly everyone was up and working. Brother David told us that the village elders were amazed at how the people got involved and that all they needed was an example to follow.

Early afternoon found us in Santa Tecla again, dropping off food and supplies. After one last organizational and planning session, we headed back to Honduras. At the border crossing, I spoke with the customs people and obtained permission to return Sunday with food and medicine to take to Vera Cruz and Ozatlan. This was necessary as the El Salvadoran government is confiscating all relief supplies that come into the country so that the government may distribute these items the way that they see fit. However, God intervened here by putting an understanding, Christian man in a place of authority in the customs office. He assured me that he would be present tomorrow that I was to find him and that he would assure our passage with the supplies to Ozatlan and Vera Cruz.

Thank you, God for Your hand in all things.

IT HELPS TO BE CRAZY!

chapter eighteen

HIKING WITH HERMAN

Herman was my best friend in Honduras and a lieutenant colonel in the army. He had invited me to do some hiking with him. Mount Celaque is the highest peak in Honduras at 10,000 feet and is visible from our home. This was where Herman had in mind for us to spend a couple of nights out, just resting and clearing our minds. I knew that I needed a break so I said let's go.

We started out a couple of days later at daybreak. From our home to where we would leave the truck was almost a two-hour drive over four-wheel-drive only roads. When we arrived at the end of the road we were met by couple of young men. These men were friends of Herman. Herman had stopped off at the local radio station in Santa Rosa the day before and left a message that was read that evening. Every evening the radio station has a time in which it relays messages to the remote villages in our part of Honduras. Herman's message asked that Pablo and his brother to meet us with a couple of burros.

After tying our packs to the animals, we started out up the mountain. Pablo and his brother would accompany us for the first mile or so. The trail took us through the jungle as it wound its way up the mountain. After a couple of hours we found ourselves in the village of El Petillo. Herman had visited the village once before and knew the chief, Juan Marcos. The village consists of about 20 houses and some 250 people.

After introductions were made we all set around under a porch for a cup of coffee. Now this village really does not see many outsiders, only a couple every few years. So, the visiting white man created quite a stir. As we talked it became known that Juan Marcos had recently made a profession of faith. He told how on his last trip down the mountain he had stopped in the village of Cucuyagua. He told of how he was walking down a trail and heard singing and praying coming from a building. He entered the building and there he found a man leading a group of people. The man then began to preach and the words touched Juan Marcos' heart. Juan Marcos told of how he had a very difficult time sleeping that night. The next morning Juan Marcos made his way back home on the mountain. That night also proved to be restless. The next morning, Juan Pablo went into the jungle and prayed to God to save him. He asked forgiveness of his sins and asked that Jesus enter his heart. This occurred just about a month before our visit. It also turned out that the building where Juan Marcos was our mission in Cucuyagua and national missionary Manuel Pinto was preaching.

Since that day when Juan Marcos accepted Christ, he had been busy. He first led his wife to Christ and then his brother. He had also constructed a building in which he was now leading a prayer time and Bible reading every evening. (Juan Marcos and his wife were the only two people in the village who could read and his wife had the only Bible in the village.) Juan Marcos had also made two visits to his mother's village, El Chimis. He was sharing with her and his other brother what he had found in God.

Now this is exciting stuff for a missionary. Here was a man who had been led to a mission, heard the Gospel and accepted the gift of salvation and then was sharing his new salvation with his family and friends.

Juan Marcos had two requests. The first was for a Bible. He said that he had been shown a Bible that had a dictionary, concordance, and other Bible study helps by Pastor Manual in Cucuyagua a couple of weeks earlier. Now, just a week earlier I had purchased a Thompson Chain Reference Bible. As I was packing the night before I put that Bible in my pack and had asked that God provide me with someone who could use that Bible. Here was God's answer. I quickly handed the Bible over. The second request was for us to accompany him to El Chimis. Herman and I quickly agreed to that.

After we finished our coffee with some beans and a couple of tortillas, Herman, Juan Marcos, and I headed out for El Chimis. For the next six and a half hours we climbed. El Chimis is located almost on the summit of the mountain. The view was beautiful. We arrived at the village just as the daily rainstorm commenced. We were ushered into the home of Paco, the brother of Juan Marcos. It turned out that we were the first outsiders to visit this village in several years and I was the first white man. So, you can imagine the commotion we created. It was not long until that small house was wall-to-wall people. Everyone had to see and to talk to the visitors. We drank more coffee and fruit juice than we could hold. We ate more beans, tortillas, and roasted iguana. It was quite a fiesta. It had been Juan Marcos' plan for us to visit and witness with his mother and family, however, the opportunity just did not present itself that evening.

By now it was dark and it was still raining. Herman and I had our hammocks so we found a dry place in the lean-to part of the barn. Needless to say, we had no problem sleeping that night. The only time that we woke up *hiking with herman*

IT HELPS TO BE CRAZY!

was when our burros started creating a ruckus, but we were both too tired to even pay much attention to that. (We found jaguar tracks within 10 yards of the barn the next morning.)

We awoke to a cloudless morning. Herman and I enjoyed some exploring on the mountaintop that day. That evening we visited more with Paco, Juan Marcos, and their mother. We also had a prayer time and impromptu Bible study. Though there was not a profession of faith, the Gospel was presented. We also heard of how Juan Marcos wanted to start a school in El Petillo. His wife had graduated from the sixth grade and was willing to act as a teacher. This was also something that we could help him with. Though content, we again slept the sleep of the tired.

The next day we traveled down the mountain and back home. We had made plans to get school materials and children's Sunday School material to Juan Marcos. We had also agreed to return to both villages in a few months.

Within a couple of weeks of our visit, Herman and I had acquired 20 small chalk slates and two large chalkboards. We also had talked the Ministry of Education into giving us books for 20 first grade students. We added other supplies to round out what was needed to get the school going. I also put a couple Sunday School Quarterlies in the shipment. Herman had detailed some soldiers to handle getting the materials up the mountain. Three weeks after our visit, Juan Marcos had his materials and the school was in session.

Nearly four months after our first trip, Herman and I went up the mountain again. My son, Joel, and a couple of teenagers from Santa Rosa accompanied us this time. When we arrived in El Petillo, there were 23 kids between the ages of six and sixteen in the church\school building. We were swamped by hugs and were blessed to hear them read a short poem in unison. They were learning to read like the kids in the big villages.

Juan Marcos was still busy. There had been 19 professions of faith in the last few months and the church building was filled every service. He had been back to Cucuyagua and had learned a few songs and hymns and now there was singing to accompany the prayer time and preaching. Juan Marcos told of how Paco had accepted the Lord the week after our visit and how his mother and six other adults were also now Believers.

We hit the trail again and were in El Chimis in good time. We pitched our tents before the rain started and enjoyed the company of our friends again. That evening we had a preaching and prayer time and two villagers accepted Christ.

IT HELPS TO BE CRAZY!

We spent another couple of days on the mountain, relaxing, and enjoying life among these new brothers and sisters. When we returned back to Santa Rosa, it was with a body refreshed, a heart rejoicing, and a soul revived.

Care to do some hiking?

chapter nineteen

A NEW WATCHMAN

Due to a few unfortunate events that occurred at our home in the night hours, it became necessary for us to acquire the services of a security company. On the first evening that the watchman was with us, I sat on the porch to visit with him; just to get to know a little about him. After a little small talk I asked him about where he attends church. Now that opened up an incredible conversation.

The watchman told me that he had attended a Catholic school as a child and teenager. He said that he had even thought of becoming a priest but his falling in love with a young lady and marrying her put an end to those ideas. However, after his marriage he was still very faithful to the Catholic Church and continued his studies with the priest and bishop. The watchman related how he had begun to teach in the diocese and to lead in many activities and ministries of the church. When he and his family moved to a smaller village, he was asked to become the lay leader of the village's congregation. This position was, in effect, a pastoral role and responsible for teaching, preaching, and caring for the parishioners as the priests and bishop rarely made it to this small village. He said that he quickly agreed.

As we were enjoying the stars and some coffee, my new friend continued his story, as his smile grew bigger and tears began to well up in his eyes. He explained that over the next year or so as he studied and taught and preached that his eyes began to be opened. He was seeing things in the Bible that did not agree with what he had been taught. Likewise, there were things that he had been told the Bible taught that he could not find anywhere in the Bible. He was realizing that many things he had heard his whole life did not match up with what he was finding in the scriptures. The watchman said that he approached the priests and the bishop with his studies and concerns. However, the bishop told him not to worry or to concern himself with what he read in the Bible but to teach what he had been taught.

Now a shaking of his head caused the teardrops to fall to the floor of the porch. "I tried to do that," he said. "But my heart and my mind would not let me say things that were not in the Bible. I could not teach that everyone was

IT HELPS TO BE CRAZY!

going to heaven, even those who did not have faith or did not live by their faith in God." He said that he approached the bishop again. The bishop told him that if he did not stop with the questioning, that he would lose his position as church leader.

The watchman related that he returned to his village disheartened. He knew that something was wrong with the teachings that he had heard since he was just a child, but he also knew that those in his church needed someone to shepherd them. "Then one evening, as I was reading in Romans, I realized that I had never prayed to Jesus," the watchman said. I really did not know who Jesus was and I did not really know him." He said that he had always thought that he would be saved because of what he did for God. The watchman said that he knelt down beside his bed and sleeping wife, prayed to Jesus for the first time in his life, and asked Jesus to forgive him and to come into his heart.

Now smiling broadly, the tears wiped away, the watchman told me how the next day he preached a message of salvation by faith and grace in the Catholic Church. He began to laugh. The bishop quickly heard of the message and other words that the watchman was now saying to the parishioners. The bishop came to the village the following week and asked the watchman if all that he had heard about the watchman was true. He told the bishop yes. The bishop excommunicated the watchman on the spot. The watchman said that he was so happy at this. He was now completely free to say what he knew was the truth. Over the next few weeks, the watchman said his wife, and several neighbors had prayed to Jesus for salvation.

It had been several months the watchman said since he had first prayed to Jesus. He said that since that night he had heard about the missionary and the evangelical church at the missionary's home, but it was too far for him and the others to visit. He explained that when he had heard that his new post was to be at the missionary's home he was so happy and thankful.

Since that first night, the watchman and I had many, many late evenings of conversation, study, and talking about God. The watchman studied with other local pastors in our local Bible Institute. And the mission that he began in his village quickly surpassed in number the Catholic Church congregation; the bishop's loss, God's gain.

Now what is it that God says about a watchman? Oh yeah, here it is...

> "Go set a watchman and let him
> declare what he sees."
>
> *Isaiah 21:6*

IT HELPS TO BE CRAZY!

chapter twenty

THE BULLET THAT BROUGHT LIFE

The Chortí people are a descendent tribe of the original Mayan people and empire. They live in the mountainous region that straddles the Honduran and Guatemalan border. For most of the nineteenth century, a conflict between the Chortí and the surrounding mestizo land owners had smoldered. The Chortí lands were prime coffee growing lands and the nearby coffee plantation owners wanted nothing more than to expand their fields into the Chortí tribal lands. The Honduran government did very little to quiet this conflict. Rather the government often seemed to add fuel to this small fire by not providing basic services, such as health clinics and schools, and the ability to vote to the Chortí. And, occasionally the conflict would flare with bullets being fired and people being hurt and killed as a plantation would attempt to extend its boundaries by encroaching into the tribe's lands.

Understandably, the Chortí had become a closed culture group. They were leery of outsiders. Their villages were hidden from and inaccessible to strangers. This fear of outsiders had also caused a barrier for religion and other cultural entities to cross over into Chortí daily life. The people's religion had changed very little, if any, over the past two thousand years. The people adored nature and their sacrifices were given to the gods of the Earth and the Wind. It is against this backdrop that this story begins.

One day I received a visit from a missionary who was living in the town of Copán. This town was where the ruins of the Mayan city of the same name were located and was the gateway town into the Chortí lands. Patrick, the missionary who was with a different mission organization, began to tell me how a representative of the Chortí had approached him and had asked Patrick if there was anyone that Patrick might know that might be able to help with providing some medical care to the Chortí people in their villages. Patrick said that we came to his mind immediately. Patrick and I then made tentative plans for a very small group of us to meet the Chortí representative and to accompany him into the Chortí reservation for a two day excursion.

Very early one morning a few weeks later, Patrick, a national pastor from the Copán area, Dalaina, my seventeen year old daughter, and I left

the bullet that brought salvation
IT HELPS TO BE CRAZY!

Copán accompanying our Chortí guide. It was very slow going along jungle roads and an hour or so later, we arrived at our first stop. We were shown the village community building and it was there that we unpacked our backpacks of medicine and rudimentary medical equipment. At first, the people were very hesitant of coming close, but they soon warmed up to us. Dalaina with her bubbly charisma and head of thick, curly hair was an attraction that few children, or adults for that matter, could withstand. With the children came their mothers. Over the course of the day we treated a couple of dozen children and women with the common ailments of parasites, respiratory infections, skin rashes and infections, and the aches and pains of living a hard physical life in culture that was not far removed from what it was two millennium earlier. (You may have noticed that I said that "we" treated the patients; that "we" included Dalaina. Dalaina had been working with me in the clinic, working with medical teams, and working in surgery at our hospital for the past four years and had become an excellent medical assistant.)

Around midmorning our guide told us that we need to pack-up our things and to follow him. No other explanation was offered, and we did not question.

After a half hour or so of travel we arrived at a cluster of a few very crude, small structures. We entered one of the huts and found a young man in his late twenties. He had been shot in the left upper leg. It was a nasty wound and was beginning to become infected. When I asked the young man why he had not gone to a clinic or the hospital he said that he was afraid to go into town. Our guide told us that those places asked too many questions and would alert the police or others with whom the Chortí did not have good relations. I explained that I would ask no further questions and that he did not have to fear us.

We carried the young man outside so that we would have better light. The operating table was two logs and large rock. A small, wooden table held our sterilized-by-iodine-and-candle instruments. Dalaina would assist me with the suturing (she could sew better than me) and I enlisted two of the young man's family to also assist. One would fan away the flies and the other would shoo the chickens and pigs from our operating suite. After I had removed the bullet and cleaned the wound and as Dalaina was doing the sewing, I had a chance to talk to this man about his life. He became very open and friendly and warmed up to me as we spoke. After a little while, I spoke to him about Christ. He said that he had heard the name Jesus but did not know anything about Christianity. He got the short version from me that afternoon.

IT HELPS TO BE CRAZY!

However, he did promise to visit with Patrick in a few days when Patrick would come back to check on him.

It was after dark when we arrived back in Copán.

The next morning, our guide took us to another village, this one much deeper into the thick, green canopied mountains. The people here were a bit more open and much more inquisitive. It was obvious that strangers like us had never visited here before. The ailments were also a bit more serious than in yesterday's villages. Though we had replenished our backpacks, the machete mishaps, severe malnourishment, tropical diseases, and serious infections were taxing our limited medical supplies. This day, it seemed as if word had gotten around about the events the previous afternoon. We also had opportunity to share about Jesus and His gospel as we visited with those who came. One older man, whom we were told was one of the village elder leaders, was very interested about Christianity. He had heard a little about the Christian God but had never read or heard of anything directly from the Bible. For some three hours that day, this man listened as we took turns reading to him a Bible that we had brought with us. After he was read some verses in the book of Romans, he was asked if he could and would place his faith in the Son of the Creator God, Jesus the Christ. He said yes and prayed his first prayer to the God that created the earth and the winds.

A couple of weeks later we heard that the young man who had been shot was now wearing the bullet we had taken from his leg around his neck. He was referring to it as the bullet that brought him salvation. This young man had accepted Christ when Patrick had visited him.

These two professions of faith were the first two among this unreached people. The testimony of these two believers and the contacts that Patrick had made on this trip was the opening of the door for the Gospel to enter into the Chortí people.

IT HELPS TO BE CRAZY!

epilogue

THE HARDEST TIME IN A MISSIONARY'S LIFE

In January of 2007, Valerie and I looked down upon the banana plantations and green mountains of Honduras as we the plane took off from what had been our home country for the past eleven years. When we surrendered to follow God's calling to become missionaries, it was our sincere intent to work ourselves out of a job. We felt, and even more so feel the same today, that believers and disciples of Christ should put the greatest emphasis into not only spreading the Gospel, but to making disciples and equipping those disciples to do the work of the church and continuing the Lord's ministries. That was what we did. We, no correct that, God, through our hands, minds, and hearts equipped the people whom we served with to take over and do the work that we were doing. In 2006, God began to let us know that our time in Central America was drawing to a close. We had witnessed an incredible harvesting of souls and unimaginable explosion of His church. It was those young men and women whom found Christ as youth and children in the Sunday School and VBS classes that we taught that were now carrying on the ministries as leaders, teachers, pastors, and missionaries. We were not needed now as we were before. Yes, we were sad, but we were also so pleased and happy. We had been so blessed to see the fruit, much fruit, more fruit, and fruit that remains, just as Christ described in John 5. But this was a hard day. The hardest days for a missionary are those days when that missionary has to follow God's leadership and walk away from the adopted homeland and the people that God had given that missionary to love and to serve. It is only by our faith in God that a missionary can survive such hard days.

As I looked over the past years since we were elected as missionaries I could see lots of victories. We had witnessed literally countless professions of faith. We had seen lives changed in ways that would bring tears to anybody's yes. We had seen children that had been given a new chance at life from once having faced starvation. We had seen people accept Christ on their deathbeds, and had seen young people give their lives to the Lord and really mean it.

epilogue
IT HELPS TO BE CRAZY!

And we had also seen some defeats, felt some pain, and had cried tears of disappointment. Not every profession of faith is for real, not every changed life stays changed, and Satan will attack anyone who is against him. We had witnessed Spiritual warfare on a personal basis.

Do we welcome this warfare, these disappointments, and the difficulties? No, but we don't shy away from them either. Remember James 1:12:

> Blessed is a man who perseveres under trial; for once he has been approved, he will receive the crown of life, which the Lord has promised to those who love Him.

This verse means that even if it is a little rough now, it will get better in the future. It means that God and His people will win!!

To be very honest, that first year or two after our return from Central America to the U.S. was very difficult. We had to adjust to a very different lifestyle. We had to find our place in the church. But the most difficult was learning the patience needed to rest as God prepared us for the next chapters in our lives of serving Him as missionaries.

And once we learned to be patient, then it was not long before God decided to let us in on what those chapters were to be.

One question that is often asked of me is, "What does one have to have to be a missionary?" A missionary has to have two things. The first necessary quality is found in 1 John 4:21:

> And this commandment we have from Him, that the one who loves God should love his brother also.

You have to love the people! If you don't love the people, don't go.

The second is that you have to be crazy enough to do things that no one else will do and to smile while you are doing them. Seeking out people who have leprosy or are demon possessed, singing praises to God in a jail cell, and getting out of a perfectly good boat to walk to take a stroll on the water are, unfortunately, things "sane" Christians do not often do. Those are things that the "crazies" do.

And when we smile while doing those crazy things, I know that God smiles with us.

www.ingramcontent.com/pod-product-compliance
Lightning Source LLC
Chambersburg PA
CBHW071314040426
42444CB00009B/2010